I0425941

March 2012

INTERAGENCY COLLABORATION

State and Army Personnel Rotation Programs Can Build on Positive Results with Additional Preparation and Evaluation

GAO

Accountability ★ Integrity ★ Reliability

GAO-12-386

GAO
Accountability * Integrity * Reliability

Highlights

Highlights of GAO-12-386, a report to congressional requesters

INTERAGENCY COLLABORATION

State and Army Personnel Rotation Programs Can Build on Positive Results with Additional Preparation and Evaluation

Why GAO Did This Study

Federal government personnel must be able to collaborate across agencies to meet complex 21st century national security challenges. GAO found in a prior report that interagency rotations are a type of professional development activity that can help improve interagency collaboration. However, government officials, policy researchers, human capital experts, and others cite many challenges to successful rotation programs.

To understand how interagency rotation programs can be designed to address these challenges, GAO was asked to (1) identify desirable collaboration-related program results; (2) identify policies and practices that help rotation programs achieve those results; and (3) determine the extent to which three rotation programs were viewed as effective and incorporated those policies and practices.

To address these objectives, GAO reviewed the literature; reviewed rotation program documents; surveyed program participants and their supervisors; and interviewed human resources experts, agency human resources practitioners, and program officials.

What GAO Recommends

GAO is making recommendations to the Secretaries of State and Defense to direct State and Army Command and General Staff College officials to build on successful efforts by establishing program evaluation processes, among other actions. Officials from both agencies reviewed a draft of this report and generally agreed with our recommendations.

View GAO-12-386. To view the e-supplement online, click GAO-12-387SP. For more information, contact J. Christopher Mihm at (202) 512-6806 or mihmj@gao.gov.

What GAO Found

Effective interagency rotational assignments can achieve collaboration-related results—such as developing participants' collaboration skills and building interagency networks—but programs must be a "win-win" for the individuals and organizations involved in order to be effective.

GAO found policies and practices that help interagency rotation programs achieve collaboration-related results as indicated in the figure below. The policies and practices addressed challenges to participation, and included incentives, preparation, and feedback.

Most participants and host supervisors of State's Foreign Policy Advisor (POLAD) program, State's other interagency rotations, and the Army Command and General Staff College (CGSC) Interagency Fellowship reported that their programs were effective in contributing to improved collaboration among agencies with national security responsibilities. The figure below also shows the extent to which these programs incorporated the policies and practices GAO identified.

Extent to Which State and Army Rotation Programs Incorporated Policies and Practices That Can Achieve Collaboration Results

Policies and practices	State POLAD	Other State rotations	CGSC Interagency Fellowship
Design the program to achieve overarching or shared strategic goals	●	◑	●
Provide individuals with incentives to participate	●	◑	●
Provide management—at the host and home agencies—with incentives to participate	●	◑	●
Optimize the match between the participant and the assignment	●	●	●
Prepare participants and their host supervisors for the rotation	●	◑	◑
Plan for participant's next assignment to maximize benefits to participant and home agency	NA[a]	○[b]	●
Create a program feedback and evaluation process that includes participants and all participating organizations	◑	○	◑

● Mostly/ fully in place
◑ Partially in place
○ Not in place
NA Not applicable

Source: GAO analysis.

[a] State's POLAD program is managed according to Foreign Service career development and staffing processes, which are based, in part, on individual initiative and preferences for subsequent assignments. Because these processes were beyond the scope of this report, GAO did not evaluate the effectiveness of how State planned for its Foreign Service participants' next assignments.

[b] GAO's finding associated with this practice is limited to the few civil service personnel that participated in other State rotations.

_____ **United States Government Accountability Office**

Contents

Figures

Abbreviations

CGSC	U.S. Army Command and General Staff College
DOD	Department of Defense
FS	Foreign Service (pay schedule)
G/FO	General/Flag Officer
GS	General Schedule
HRC	U.S. Army Human Resources Command
JPME	Joint Professional Military Education
MOA	Memorandum of Agreement
MOU	Memorandum of Understanding
NSPD	National Security Professional Development
O	Officer level
POLAD	Foreign Policy Advisor
QDDR	Quadrennial Diplomacy and Development Review
SES	Senior Executive Service
SFS	Senior Foreign Service
State	Department of State
TRADOC	U.S. Army Training and Doctrine Command
USMS	United States Marshals Service

View GAO-12-386 key component

Interagency Collaboration: Survey Results of State and Army Personnel Rotation Program Participants and Their Host-Agency Supervisors (GAO-12-387SP), an e-supplement to GAO-12-386

March 9, 2012

Congressional Requesters

The complex national security challenges of the 21st century—such as nuclear proliferation, global pandemics, and terrorist attacks—require a U.S. federal government workforce that can collaborate effectively across agency lines. Congress is considering using interagency rotation programs—which we previously identified as one type of professional development activity that can help improve interagency collaboration—to promote collaboration across the federal national security workforce.[1] The Interagency Personnel Rotation Act of 2011, pending before the Senate and House, would encourage interagency rotations by requiring interagency experience for national security and homeland security personnel prior to promotion to certain senior positions.[2]

There is broad agreement that although interagency rotations can help to build bridges between the myriad agencies involved in national security, there are many challenges to the success of interagency rotation programs.[3] For example, an individual may be deterred from participating because of the perception that interagency rotations can slow or derail career advancement. From the agency perspective, there may be reluctance to send participants on rotation because of the potential negative effect on its workforce capacity, or to host participants who may take too much time to bring up to speed.

To better understand how to effectively design and implement interagency rotation programs and overcome these challenges, you

---

[1] GAO, *National Security: An Overview of Professional Development Activities Intended to Improve Interagency Collaboration*, GAO-11-108 (Washington, D.C.: Nov. 15, 2011).

[2] See S. 1268 and H.R. 2314. The purpose of these acts is to increase the efficiency and effectiveness of the government by fostering greater interagency experience among executive branch personnel on national security and homeland security matters involving more than one agency.

[3] See GAO-11-108; Project on National Security Reform, *The Power of People: Building an Integrated National Security Professional System for the 21st Century* (Washington, D.C.: November 2010); and Congressional Research Service, *National Security Professionals and Interagency Reform: Proposals, Recent Experience, and Issues for Congress*, RL34565, (Washington, D.C.: Sept. 26, 2011).

asked us to (1) identify desirable collaboration-related program results—in terms of individual competencies and organizational results; (2) identify policies and practices that help interagency rotation programs achieve collaboration-related results; and (3) determine the extent to which three rotation programs were viewed as effective and incorporated those policies and practices.

To address these objectives, we took several approaches. To identify desirable collaboration-related program results and policies and practices to achieve those results, we drew on three sources of information:

- We conducted a review of literature, including academic articles, trade publications, and other sources.

- We interviewed and then administered a follow-up questionnaire to federal human capital and training and development practitioners at 9 agencies with national security responsibilities (agency practitioners). The practitioners included agency officials from the three programs we reviewed.

- We interviewed human capital and training and development experts external to the 9 national security agencies (external experts). We identified these external experts by seeking referrals from human capital and professional development practitioners at GAO and from professional associations, such as the National Academy of Human Resources and the National Academy for Public Administration, and other experts.

From these three sources of information, we extracted (1) positive results that can generally be achieved by rotation programs and (2) effective policies and practices for achieving these results. To identify the most important results, policies, and practices, we analyzed them according to how frequently they were cited and whether they appeared in one, two, or all three sources of information. We also included just those results, policies, and practices that were relevant to the federal government.

Based on our prior work, we identified three interagency rotation programs operating in the federal national security arena. Two are at the

Department of State (State) and one is at the U.S. Army Command and General Staff College (CGSC) within the Department of Defense (DOD).[4]

To determine the extent to which the State and DOD interagency rotation programs incorporated the policies and practices we identified, and to assess the effectiveness of these programs in achieving desirable collaboration-related results, we reviewed program documents, interviewed responsible agency officials, and administered a survey to all fiscal year 2009 participants and their supervisors both prior to their rotations, if relevant,[5] and at the host agency.[6] We received a sufficient response from participants and host agency supervisors to report their views.[7] We did not receive a sufficient response from prior agency supervisors to reflect the views of those supervisors and therefore do not report those results.

We conducted this performance audit from February 2011 to March 2012 in accordance with generally accepted government auditing standards. Those standards require that we plan and perform the audit to obtain sufficient, appropriate evidence to provide a reasonable basis for our findings and conclusions based on our audit objectives. We believe that the evidence obtained provides a reasonable basis for our findings and conclusions based on our audit objectives.

---

[4]In GAO-11-108, we identified seven interagency rotational assignment programs intended to improve national security collaboration while providing professional development opportunities for its participants. We excluded those from our review that were newly established and/or those that targeted participants without prior professional experience, such as military school cadets, since it would be difficult to gauge whether these programs had contributed to organizational results or to participants' professional development.

[5]Because the DOD program at the Army CGSC sends participants directly from an academic program to an interagency rotational assignment, these participants did not have line supervisors immediately prior to their participation.

[6]We asked agency officials to identify all rotational assignment participants in fiscal year 2009 and all of the host agency individuals that supervised participants in 2009. Because some assignments last for up to three years, some participants may have continued their rotational assignment through 2010 or beyond.

[7]We received responses from 77 of 124 (62 percent) participants, 41 of 85 (48 percent) host supervisors, and 21 of 58 (36 percent) prior supervisors. See appendix I for additional information on the survey.

Background

Interagency rotation programs, or interagency rotations, are work assignments at a different agency from the one in which the participant is normally employed, with an explicit professional development purpose. As we previously reported, several federal agencies have used interagency rotations to help accomplish their national security missions while also explicitly seeking to develop participants' abilities to collaborate on national security.[8]

State Foreign Policy Advisor Program

The State Foreign Policy Advisor (POLAD) program is a 1- to 3-year rotation that places State Foreign Service Officers at the Pentagon or at military commands to work alongside DOD civilians and military officers. These include Foreign Policy Advisors, State-Defense Exchange Officers, and State positions with Joint Interagency Coordination Groups.[9] The POLAD program seeks to provide participants with opportunities to develop their knowledge of military culture, roles, and responsibilities, while providing a foreign policy perspective to military planning and operations. These assignments also are to provide opportunities to establish networks between diplomats and military staff who must work together on global issues. These rotations target mid- to senior-level State Foreign Service Officers. Formally established in the early 1960s, the POLAD program was created to further coordination between State and DOD and to ensure that both diplomatic and military strategies were employed to address national security challenges. State officials told us that, over time, they found that the POLAD program also had become a means for developing Foreign Service Officers' experience and effectiveness in operating in a military environment. The size of the program is also expanding: during the past 4 years, the number of diplomats serving in these positions has more than doubled, to near 90.

---

[8]GAO-11-108.

[9]Joint Interagency Coordination Groups, housed within DOD combatant commands, are intended to serve as a coordinating body among the civilian agencies in Washington, D.C., the country ambassadors, the combatant commands' staffs, and other multinational and multilateral bodies within the region.

State Interagency Rotations at Other Government Agencies and Federal Learning Institutes	These assignments are 1- to 3-year rotations that place State Foreign Service and civil service personnel at federal agencies or federal learning institutions. Participants are to have opportunities to learn about the roles and responsibilities of the host agencies and to establish professional networks with personnel from different agencies working on similar issues. These rotations target mid- to senior-level State Foreign Service Officers and civil service employees, depending on the position. While these assignments are not part of a formal program, State has been sending personnel on assignments to some of the same organizations, such as the National Defense University or the National Security Staff, for more than a decade. In State's most recent announcement for interagency rotation positions available in 2012-2013, they identified rotations to 8 federal organizations, which represented approximately 45 positions.[10]
Army Command and General Staff College Intermediate Level Education Interagency Fellowship Program	The Interagency Fellowship Program is a 10- to 12-month rotation that places Army officers in intermediate-level positions at other federal agencies and allows them to learn the culture of the host agency, hone collaborative skills such as communication and teamwork, and establish networks with their civilian counterparts. The program targets field-grade Army officers, primarily majors. First piloted in 2008, the program was designed to achieve multiple objectives. These interagency assignments are to provide Fellows with valuable developmental experiences while they increase workforce capacity at their host civilian agencies, such as State and U.S. Agency for International Development. In turn, the civilian agencies can free up resources to send civilian personnel to teach or attend courses at Army Command and General Staff College (CGSC). The Interagency Fellowship program had 23 participants in 2009 and 26 in 2010. In the current program year, there are 28.

---

[10]The announcement did not specify the precise number of positions at each organization, since some were conditional on funding availability.

Effective Interagency Rotation Programs Achieve Collaboration-Related Results for Individuals and Organizations

As we have previously reported, collaborative approaches to national security require a well-trained workforce with the skills and experience to integrate the government's diverse capabilities and resources.[11] According to our analysis of the literature and the perspectives of external experts and agency practitioners, effective interagency rotations help achieve collaboration-related results by improving the participant's knowledge of other agencies, building the participant's leadership and collaboration skills and experience, and offering the participant opportunities to form interagency networks. The participant's home agency can increase its capacity to collaborate by leveraging the participant's experience. In addition, the home agency can ensure that it has an adequate supply of current and future leaders with the broad perspectives, collaboration skills, and other competencies necessary to succeed in an interagency environment. The participant's host agency can benefit from the temporary increase in workforce capacity, as well as from applying the participant's particular skills, experiences, or other characteristics to a specific mission or project. In addition, the host agency can build its network with the home agency, using its relationship with the participant for future collaboration once he or she has returned to the home agency.

As one expert explained, designing a rotation so that it is a "win-win" for the individual participants and organizations involved is critical to its success. Of the 34 federal human capital and training officials that responded to our post-interview questionnaire, 33 agreed that it was important for interagency rotations to provide developmental opportunities for individual participants while helping the host agency meet its mission responsibilities. The same number also agreed that the home agency should benefit (e.g., be able to achieve mission objectives more effectively) from the knowledge, skills, and professional networks that participants develop during rotations (see figure 1).

---

[11]GAO, *Interagency Collaboration: Key Issues for Congressional Oversight of National Security Strategies, Organizations, Workforce, and Information Sharing*, GAO-09-904SP (Washington, D.C.: Sept. 25, 2009).

Figure 1: Effective Interagency Rotations Achieve Collaboration-Related Results for Individuals and Organizations

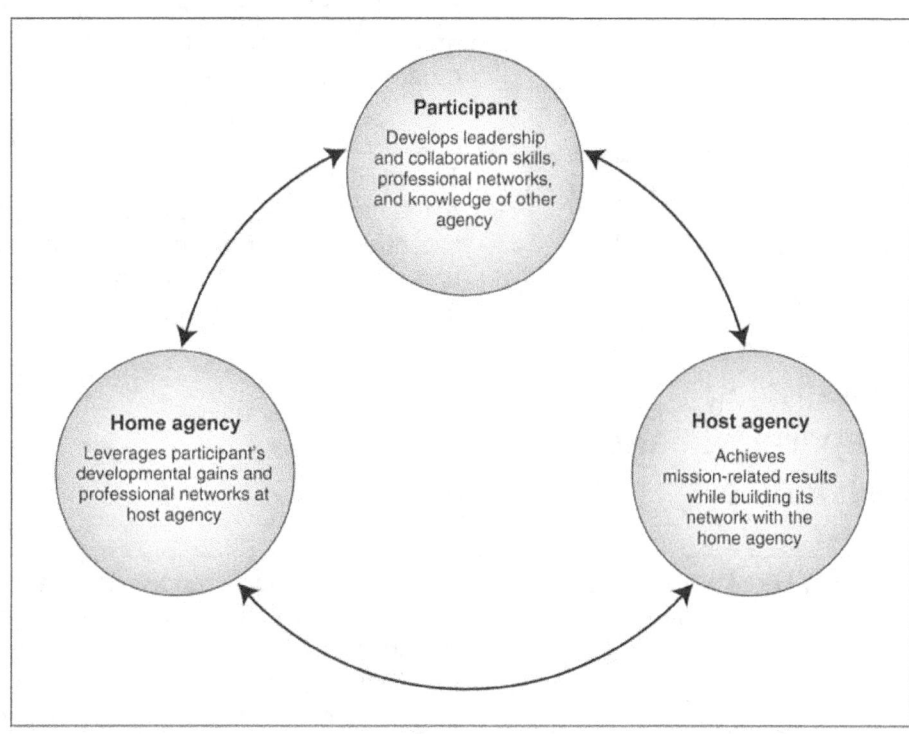

Source: GAO.

Although interagency rotation programs can bring about these positive results for all involved parties, our analysis indicates that there are challenges to the success of these programs. For example, there are potential costs to participants' career progression, due to time away from the home agency or other factors. Rotation programs, if not managed effectively, can also temporarily diminish the home organizations' workforce capacities. As one human capital official noted, in the face of diminishing resources, managers may become even more reluctant to let their high performers go on interagency rotations.

Moreover, our prior work has shown that to improve interagency collaboration, agencies need to address factors beyond those associated with workforce collaboration abilities. For example, organizational differences—including differences in organizational structures, planning processes, and funding sources—between and among multiple agencies can also hinder collaboration.[12] Many of the experts we interviewed agreed that to bring about improved interagency collaboration, rotation programs must be part of a larger strategy that addresses such organizational factors.

Effective Interagency Rotation Programs Support Shared Goals and Incorporate Incentives, Preparation, and Feedback

The policies and practices described below are the result of our analysis of the literature and the perspectives of external experts and agency practitioners we interviewed. According to that analysis, these policies and practices can help interagency rotational programs achieve collaboration-related results.

Design the Program to Achieve Overarching or Shared Strategic Goals

We have previously reported that agencies should undertake strategic workforce planning to identify the workforce they need to accomplish their current and future mission. Such planning should involve identifying the necessary competencies, size, and deployment of the workforce as well as any current or future gaps. Training and development activities, such as interagency rotations, should be designed to fill these gaps so that the agency can more effectively achieve its strategic goals.[13] Thus, for interagency rotation programs to be effective in bringing about collaboration-related results, they should be designed to help achieve the agency's collaboration-dependent goals and, ideally, cross-organizational goals. In linking the program to overarching or shared strategic goals, agencies should make the case that the benefits of interagency rotations outweigh the costs to the organization as a whole, which can help to address management concerns regarding the program.

---

[12]GAO, *Results-Oriented Government: Practices That Can Help Enhance and Sustain Collaboration among Federal Agencies*, GAO-06-15 (Washington, D.C.: Oct. 21, 2005).

[13] GAO, *Human Capital: Key Principles for Effective Strategic Workforce Planning*, GAO-04-39 (Washington, D.C.: Dec. 11, 2003).

Provide Individuals with Incentives to Participate

To ensure a rotation program's success, steps should be taken to address any real or perceived disincentives to participate and to attract the agencies' strongest candidates. For example, potential applicants may fear that they will be "out of sight, out of mind" while on rotation, and that their performance reviews will not adequately reflect their experiences at the host agency. We found that the following incentives may encourage participation:

- **Harness internal motivations:** Prospective rotation program participants may be motivated by personal interest, beliefs, or other intrinsic factors. As a human capital expert we spoke with noted, one way to encourage individuals to take assignments outside of their home organization is to tap into their desire "to do the right thing." If an organization can articulate how and why a rotation is for the greater good, it can serve as a powerful incentive. Many of our participant survey respondents described internal motivating factors—such as opportunities to work in new environments or to help host agencies to achieve national security goals—as "very important" to them in deciding to participate in their programs.[14]

- **Use performance management systems:** Agencies should ensure that they have the means to recognize and reward accomplishments and good performance outside the home agency. Agencies can provide management with guidance on how to consider performance on rotation when conducting performance appraisals. They can also consider adding a collaboration-related competency or performance standard—or modifying an existing competency or standard to include collaboration—against which individual performance can be rated.

- **Factor rotations into promotion decisions:** Personnel may be encouraged to participate in rotation programs if agencies factor interagency experience into their promotion decisions. In the military services, the requirement to have joint duty experience prior to promotion to general and flag officer ranks is often cited as a key incentive put in place to encourage participation in assignments across service or agency boundaries. However, as several experts on civil service management cautioned, there are potential challenges to

---

[14]We did not survey individuals who were eligible for these rotational assignment programs but chose not to participate. Factors that might have motivated them to participate may be different from the factors described here.

establishing interagency rotations as a promotion requirement. For example, sufficient rotation opportunities must be available and safeguards should be put in place to ensure the selection process for rotation participants is fair.

- **Provide public recognition:** In addition to providing incentives through performance management systems, agencies can publicly acknowledge or reward participants in other ways. For example, agencies could confer awards to individuals who exhibit exemplary teamwork skills or accomplishments during an interagency rotation. On a less formal level, agency leaders could invite returning participants to present information on their host agency's culture, organization, or operating methods to agency management and peers. While this less formal approach is not necessarily related to the individual participant's performance, it does allow agency leadership to signal the value of participating in interagency rotations, which can encourage others to participate in the future.

Provide Management—at Host and Home Agencies—with Incentives to Participate

Management, both at the senior leadership and immediate supervisor level, can significantly influence an interagency rotation program's success. We found that programs and their home organizations can create participation incentives through some of the following practices:

- **Agency leadership articulates benefits of and demonstrates long-term commitment to interagency rotations:** Agency leaders can work to ensure that managers understand the value of the program to the agency or to the government as a whole. This is important for getting buy-in from senior managers, who are most likely to bear the direct costs of the program, such as the temporary loss of an employee or the time a rotating employee needs to acclimate to the agency. As one expert stated, the leadership sets the tone for rotations which can encourage managers to allow for these assignments. In addition, widespread leadership support of the program may help to ensure that its sponsorship will endure through leadership changes.

- **Agencies identify and agree upon interagency governance mechanisms:** We have reported that integrating the efforts of national security agencies and related programs has proven challenging.[15] To minimize coordination issues that can make a rotation difficult or time-consuming to manage, agencies should have an interagency governance mechanism that clearly defines organizational and individual roles and responsibilities. For example, agencies can use memorandums of agreement to address considerations such as how participants will be selected, which agency pays salary and any relocation costs, and how performance accountability will be managed. Governance agreements can also be used to describe how challenges will be addressed and involved parties are to be held accountable. For example, one expert described an agreement for a rotational exchange program, where two organizations would swap managers, thereby ensuring that neither organization would have a hole in a key management position. Another expert noted that agreements can also address accountability mechanisms to ensure that both organizations are sending high-performers, with provisions to terminate the exchange early if expectations were not met. Our analysis indicated that whether a rotation is structured as an exchange or not, providing host-agency management with a formal role in appraising a participant's performance is key to addressing potential concerns with performance accountability.

- **Agency performance management systems reward managers for supporting interagency rotations:** To help engender cultures in which interagency rotations are valued, agencies can create incentives for managers to develop their personnel and share their human resources. Agency officials indicated that managers may be concerned that their highest-performing staff may be recruited away from them or that they will lose limited resources to a long detail. The performance management system is one tool agencies can use to create the expectations that managers must be willing to share their talent and those who share talent will be rewarded. For example, some private sector companies include an explicit goal in their senior executive performance agreements regarding sharing and rotating staff resources. By rewarding managers for supporting interagency rotations and contributing to enterprisewide goals, agencies can nurture a culture where rotations are valued.

---

[15]GAO, *Interagency Collaboration: Key Issues for Congressional Oversight of National Security Strategies, Organizations, Workforce, and Information Sharing,* GAO-09-904SP (Washington, D.C.: Sept. 25, 2009).

- **Agencies provide host-agency management with high-performing participants:** Host-agency managers will continue to be willing to host participants if the participants are consistently high performers. There are several practices that can help control participant quality. Many sources we reviewed indicated that identifying candidates through an open application process and evaluating or ranking them against specific criteria—competitive selection—is an effective practice. For example, experts suggested that, at minimum, only candidates with satisfactory performance appraisals should be considered. A related practice is to widely publicize program opportunities to reach the greatest number of qualified applicants.

Optimize the Match between the Participant and the Assignment

To maximize the benefits of the program to the participant, the host agency, and the home agency, rotation programs should place rotating employees in positions that best use their unique skill sets and help them to develop professionally while addressing host agency needs.

- **Ensure host-agency needs are taken into account in defining assignments:** Experts indicated that placing participants in positions for which they were not qualified or could not contribute to host organization goals could negatively affect host-agency support for the program, which is crucial to its success. Host-agencies' needs can be taken into account by having them contribute to the rotation's position description or qualifications or having them participate in the selection of candidates, among other ways.

- **Ensure participants' developmental needs are taken into account in assigning positions:** To ensure that participants will acquire the skills and experiences needed for the next level of management in their organizations, programs should have a process for reviewing candidates' developmental needs and matching them with positions that would suit them. For example, agencies could require that candidates submit their individual development plans or detail in their application how the rotation will help them to address their developmental needs.

Prepare Participants and Their Host Supervisors for the Rotation

To maximize the benefit of the interagency rotation, agencies should prepare participants and their host supervisors. In addition, the goals of the assignment should be clearly defined and communicated to all parties.

- **Provide orientation training or materials:** Orientation training or materials can help to minimize the learning curve inherent in joining a new organization and allow the participant to contribute meaningfully to the host organization sooner. Preparing the host-agency supervisor is also important. As one expert noted, without some guidance and support, it can be difficult for supervisors to successfully manage the assignment. Orientation materials could include information on the goals of the program, roles and responsibilities of the participant and supervisor, key aspects of the host agency's structure, mission, and responsibilities, as well as the administrative aspects of rotating, such as how to be reimbursed for travel expenses. In addition, orientation materials could address how host supervisors can maximize the rotation experience.

- **Define and communicate goals for the assignment:** It is important for participants and host-agency supervisors to have the same understanding of the purpose of the assignment and the participant's responsibilities. Having a clear understanding of the goals for the interagency rotation will help the participant to better understand his or her role at the agency and how he or she will be evaluated. To help encourage a discussion of the goals of the rotation among relevant parties, agencies could develop a checklist of the topics to be discussed between participants and their host agency supervisors.

Plan for Participant's Next Assignment to Maximize Benefits to Participant and Home Agency

Effective interagency rotation programs plan for a participant's next assignment to ensure that the valuable professional development the participant gained through these time- and resource-intensive rotations is not squandered. Moreover, when a participant's post-rotation responsibilities fail to build on his or her developmental experience, the participant may be dissatisfied, and as a result, more likely to leave the organization.

- **Home agencies can leverage participant gains in a variety of ways:** Agencies can assign participants to positions that directly benefit from their interagency experience and developmental gains. If such assignments or responsibilities are not available, agencies could have participants write and share white papers on their experiences or present briefings to interested agency officials and colleagues. External experts that we spoke with indicated that if the knowledge, skills, and networks gained through an interagency rotation are not used in the short-term, they can be lost or become irrelevant. One expert noted that professional networks are particularly vulnerable to obsolescence, as contacts move to new positions and responsibilities shift. According to several experts, being strategic in selecting the initial rotation assignment can help to sustain networks after the assignment is over; rotating participants across agencies but within communities of practice, such as disaster response or post-conflict reconstruction, is one way to address this.

- **Encourage periodic contact between participant and home agency to discuss post-program responsibilities:** Periodic contact between the participant and home agency helps the participant transition back to the permanent position or on to the next assignment, and helps the home agency leverage the participant's new skills. By maintaining contact, agencies are able to better identify the participant's skills, knowledge, and networks and can plan in advance how to make the best use of them. In addition, occasional contact between the participant and home agency can also improve the home agency's ability to retain participants after rotation, which some agency officials we interviewed cited as a concern of home agency managers. Contact between the participant and the home agency can also help to allay participants' concerns that their home-agency management will forget them while on rotation.

Create a Program Feedback and Evaluation Process That Includes Participants and All Participating Organizations

Our prior work has shown that evaluation is a key component of any training and development program that should occur throughout the development and implementation process.[16] Collecting feedback on the program from both the participant and host agency supervisor perspectives can help to build on lessons learned and improve the program. In addition, such evaluations can also help to demonstrate the impact and success of the program. One commonly accepted program evaluation model consists of five levels of assessment that measure (1) participant reaction to the training program; (2) changes in employee skills, knowledge, or abilities; (3) changes in on-the-job behaviors; (4) the impact of the training on program or organizational results; and (5) a return on investment that compares training costs to derived benefits. However, not all levels of evaluation are appropriate for all types of programs. In particular, the complexity and cost of conducting the more rigorous evaluations must be weighed in terms of the program's significance and cost. At minimum, to achieve a balanced approach,

---

[16]GAO, *Human Capital: A Guide for Training and Development Efforts in the Federal Government*, GAO-04-546G (Washington, D.C.: March 2004).

agencies should gather feedback from individual stakeholders as well as consider organizational results.[17] See figure 2 for some examples of rotational program elements that can be evaluated.

Figure 2: Examples of Interagency Rotation Program Elements That Can Be Evaluated

Evaluations can be conducted at different times during the course of the rotational assignment program. While there are a range of program elements that can be assessed, our analysis indicates that at minimum, it is critical to collect information from participants and the home and host agency management. Some experts recommend additional sources of evaluation data, depending on the dimension of program effectiveness being reviewed. The list below shows selected program evaluation elements prepared by a working group of the Conference Board, a research organization that supports management and performance improvements among global corporations.

Rotation Participant Preparation
- Orientation evaluation
- Participant self-assessment

Upon Completion of the Rotation
- Performance appraisal of rotation participant
- Surveys with host and home agencies, participants, and supervisors
- Feedback or interviews with rotation participant and host agency supervisor
- Analysis of achievement of outcome performance measures
- 360 degree feedback

After 2-3 Years of Rotations
- Interviews with graduated rotation participants and their current managers
- Surveys with host and home agencies, participants, and supervisors
- Analysis of rotation participants:
  o Retention rate of rotation participants
  o Diversity of rotation participants
  o Current performance and performance ratings of rotation participants
  o Promotion rates of rotation participants
- Cost value analysis

Source: GAO analysis of The Conference Board findings.

---

[17]GAO-04-546G.

State and DOD Rotation Programs Viewed As Effective in Achieving Results; and Incorporated or Partially Incorporated Most Desirable Policies and Practices

The majority of participants and supervisors who responded to our survey rated their programs as very effective in achieving collaboration-related results (see figure 3).[18]

Figure 3: Responses of Participants and Host Supervisors to the Survey Question "How effective, if at all, is the interagency rotational assignment program in contributing to improved collaboration among agencies with national security responsibilities?"

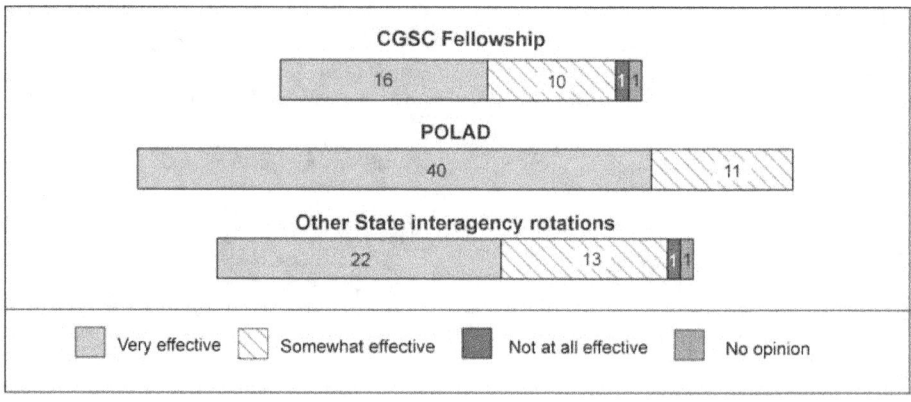

Source: GAO.

Both participants and supervisors were asked open-ended questions about the outcomes of the programs. Of the participants and supervisors who responded to these questions, the majority (20 of 25 host supervisors and 46 of 55 participants) provided examples of positive outcomes, or generally wrote positive comments about the programs. Several of these comments (4 host supervisors and 7 participants) reflected the perspective that interagency collaboration is necessary. One participant and one host supervisor described negative outcomes, which in both cases, appeared to reflect a poor match between the participant and the host organization.

---

[18]Host supervisors and participants for each program responded to several questions on collaboration-related outcomes that could be achieved through the programs. Responses to all questions were mostly positive, with at least 85 percent responding either "very effective" or "somewhat effective." Results for all questions of the two surveys are available in GAO-12-387SP, the e-supplement to this report.

Selected Survey Responses on Additional Program Outcomes

"There is no substitute for working in the actual environment of another agency. IA [interagency] task forces don't even come close."
--POLAD participant

"Following my rotation to Department of State, I deployed ... to a [redacted] unit. The contacts and processes that I learned ... [while on rotation] were extremely helpful and benefited the mission."
--Army CGSC Interagency Fellow

"Because our job involves working in both the political and military realms [our POLAD] keeps us very engaged and aware of State policies, positions, and provides insights, as we develop programs, that keep us in line with our interagency partner positions."
--host supervisor to POLAD

"[Other outcomes of the program are] better critical thinking skills about the challenges in US security environment. Broader perspective."
--State interagency rotation participant

Source: GAO survey responses.

Based on our analysis of program documents, interviews with program officials, and responses to our survey of program participants and supervisors, we found that State's POLAD and other rotation programs and Army's CGSC Interagency Fellowship program incorporated or partially incorporated most of the policies and practices that can help achieve collaboration-related results. The exceptions were post-rotation planning and program evaluation processes at State (See figure 4).

Figure 4: Extent to Which State and Army Rotation Programs Incorporated Policies and Practices that Can Achieve Collaboration Results

Policies and practices	State POLAD	Other State rotations	CGSC Interagency Fellowship
Design the program to achieve overarching or shared strategic goals	●	◑	●
Provide individuals with incentives to participate	●	◑	●
Provide management—at the host and home agencies-with incentives to participate	●	◑	●
Optimize the match between the participant and the assignment	●	●	●
Prepare participants and their host supervisors for the rotation	●	◑	◑
Plan for participant's next assignment to maximize benefits to participant and home agency	NAᵃ	○ᵇ	●
Create a program feedback and evaluation process that includes participants and all participating organizations	◑	○	◑

● Mostly/ fully in place

◑ Partially in place

○ Not in place

NA Not applicable

Source: GAO analysis.

[a]State's POLAD program is managed according to Foreign Service career development and staffing processes, which are based, in part, on individual initiative and preferences for subsequent assignments. Because these processes were beyond the scope of this report, we did not evaluate the effectiveness of how State planned for its Foreign Service participants' next assignments.

[b]Our finding associated with this practice is limited to the few civil service personnel that participated in other State rotations.

State's POLAD Program Was Created to Achieve Collaboration-Related National Security Goals

To be effective, interagency rotation programs should be designed as part of an organization's strategic goals or cross-organizational goals. We found that State's POLAD program was initially created to achieve specific goals shared by State and DOD and has continued to evolve in scope and purpose. The 2010-2015 Quadrennial Diplomacy and Development Review (QDDR), a high-level assessment and planning blueprint for State and the U.S. Agency for International Development, notes the role and importance of interagency rotations in improving coordination. At the agency level, a key planning document for State's Bureau of Political-Military Affairs—its fiscal year 2013 Strategic and Resource Plan—specifically links the POLAD program to the Bureau's strategic goals. In addition, the memorandum of understanding (MOU) between DOD and State for these interagency rotations states that "the long-standing practice of detailing personnel between these two agencies has greatly facilitated coordination" in helping to achieve the agencies' "shared responsibility for national security and the need to coordinate carefully on numerous issues affecting both foreign policy and defense."

Selected Survey Responses From POLAD Host Supervisors

"This is a superb program that should continue and if funding permits, be expanded. It is an excellent way to establish the basis for ongoing inter-agency cooperation."

"The world in which we work and the issues we face do not lend themselves any longer to single federal agency solutions. Interagency cooperation and coordination are essential for improving the US governments overall capability to accomplish our national security objectives. Interagency assignments must become the norm, not the exception. The [redacted] relationship between DOD and DOS is a good model."

Source: GAO survey responses.

State Provided Incentives for Participation in the POLAD Program through Human Resources Management Policies and Public Acknowledgment

We found that State had put in place several of the policies and practices that can provide incentives for individuals to participate in the POLAD program. In fiscal year 2008, State revised its Foreign Service Officer competencies—used in performance appraisals for promotion and tenure purposes—to include interagency experience.[19] Specifically, the competencies now identify knowledge of other agencies and interagency cooperation among the skill sets to be assessed. In addition, the first QDDR, released publicly in 2010, acknowledged the important role that POLAD participants play in helping to coordinate regional responses in

---

[19]Foreign Service terminology for competencies are "precepts," which according to State documentation, define "the specific skills to be considered and the level of accomplishment expected at different grades."

the field and allowing for successful partnering with DOD at the combatant commands. Agency officials said that these changes have resulted in increased interest in POLAD assignments, demonstrated by the increase in the number of applicants to the program in recent years. Moreover, the POLAD program publishes stories featuring POLAD participants and their experiences in an internal newsletter.

State Provided Incentives for POLAD Supervisors to Participate through Its Program Application and Selection Process

We found that State provides incentives to DOD to host POLADs by seeking to provide high-performing participants.[20] The vacancy announcements for POLAD positions are widely publicized through an annual cable to a State Department-wide audience and then posted through the regular Foreign Service assignment process, to ensure a broad applicant pool. Most POLAD participants responding to our survey indicated that they were aware of efforts to market or publicize the program (30 of 37). POLAD candidates are subject to a competitive selection process. Moreover, State involves DOD in the candidate vetting and selection process, which is subject to DOD consultation and concurrence. All of the 15 POLAD host supervisors that responded to our survey were either very satisfied (12) or somewhat satisfied (3) with the quality of the participant. Most of the 15 were very satisfied (9) or somewhat satisfied (3) with his/her role in the selection of the participant.

POLAD Program Accounted for DOD Needs and Took Steps to Consider Candidates' Developmental Needs in Matching Candidates to Assignments

We found that State has several policies and practices in place intended to meet DOD's needs. There is a provision in the MOU between DOD and State allowing for review of the POLAD positions every two years, to ensure their continued relevance. As another means of ensuring that the POLAD participant is a good match for DOD's needs, according to State POLAD program management, they work directly with the military commands to get as much detail as possible to develop the position description.

---

[20]According to State officials, because POLAD program participants are Foreign Service officers, who are expected to move onward from assignment to assignment, their participation in interagency rotations does not disadvantage their supervisors by leaving temporary workforce gaps. We therefore we did not review whether State provides incentives for supervisors of prospective POLADs to support them in going on interagency rotations.

State has taken some steps to consider the POLAD candidates' developmental needs when assessing applications. State officials described the one-page biographic statement, which is part of the POLAD application process, as a source of information on the applicants' developmental needs and goals. They also noted that candidates can submit resumes and similar material as part of their application, which can help POLAD program management to understand how their assignment history might fit with the position. Most POLAD participants and all host agency supervisors that completed our survey indicated that they were somewhat or very satisfied with the match between the participants' abilities and the assignment (33 of 37 POLAD participants; 15 of 15 host agency supervisors).

POLAD Program Provided Orientation for Participants and Has Begun to Offer Preparatory Materials to Host Supervisors

To prepare POLAD participants for the assignment, State provides a 2- to 3-day participant orientation that provides background information on DOD structure and culture as well tips for success in the POLAD assignment, among other topics. Participants are provided with an orientation handbook, which includes advice for adapting to the military environment; an overview of DOD's organizational culture, as well as its military structure and operations; advice from previous POLADs; and a listing of each year's POLAD assignees. A program official said they encourage new POLAD participants to connect with experienced POLAD participants to seek out preparatory advice.

The majority of POLAD participants responding to our survey indicated that they received orientation training and materials and thought that it was sufficient (see figure 5).[21] In addition, in 2010 and 2011 the POLAD program conducted an assessment of its orientation session so as to identify any needed modifications and improve outreach and publicity. A POLAD program official said that that these orientation evaluations are now required and noted that the program intends to expand the scope of the evaluation in 2012 to contact the previous year's participants for their feedback.

---

[21] See GAO-12-387SP, the e-supplement to this report, for complete list of questions pertaining to orientation training and materials that respondents answered.

Figure 5: Responses of POLAD Participants to the Questions "Did you take part in an orientation or training intended to prepare you for your interagency rotational assignment?" and "Were you provided with written guidance or other materials intended to prepare you for your interagency rotational assignment?"

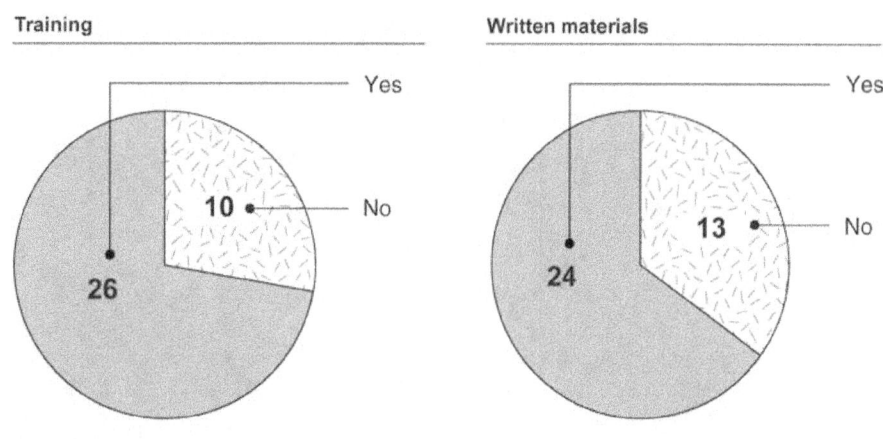

Training

Written materials

Source: GAO.

According to a State official, the POLAD program will provide orientation materials specifically targeted to host agency supervisors upon request. In addition, the orientation session for participants is open to host-agency supervisors on a space-available basis. This official also noted that program management regularly reviews job announcements for generals and flag officers at commands where POLADs are assigned, in order to identify any leadership turnover. When this occurs, program management contacts the incoming commander with background information about the POLAD program and offers additional information or materials, although the State official said that, to date, no one has accepted the offer. This is consistent with our survey results, in which few of the host supervisors responding to our survey indicated that they were provided with written guidance or other materials to prepare them to supervise a POLAD participant, as shown in figure 6.

Figure 6: Responses of POLAD Host Supervisors to the Questions "Did you take part in an orientation or training intended to prepare you to host a participant?" and "Were you provided with written guidance or other materials intended to prepare you to host a participant?"

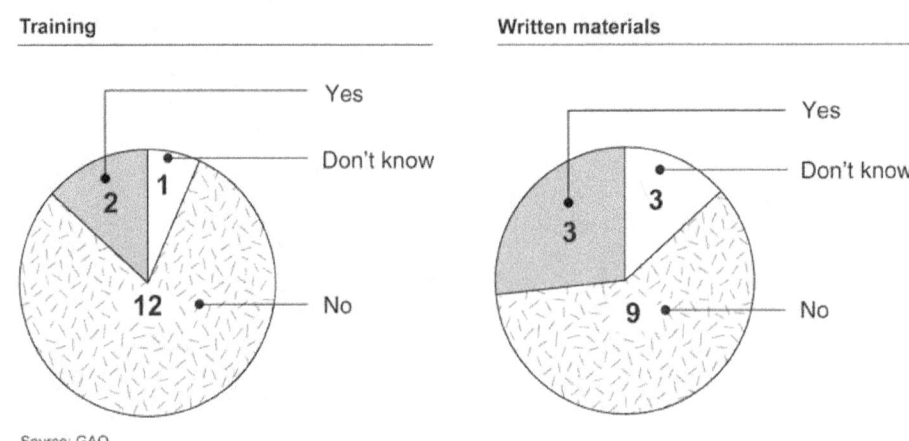

Source: GAO.

Agency officials explained that the majority of host supervisors are high-ranking DOD officials who have been working with POLAD participants for years and do not need any preparation to supervise a POLAD. However, not all of the host agency supervisors have had prior experience with the POLAD program. One host supervisor commented in a survey response that supervisors with less experience with the program may benefit from training or information on how best to employ the participant. Another wrote that even though there may be program information provided in the D.C. area, this information does not always "trickle down" to field locations. Two participants wrote that it would have been useful if their host agency had been offered training or instruction regarding their role as POLAD participants. During the course of our review, POLAD program management developed a briefing on the POLAD program for host agency supervisors at the DOD commands. The briefing included information on program goals, participant and host-agency roles and responsibilities, and other topics that we identified as useful preparatory information.

POLAD Program Has Taken Steps to Collect Feedback But Did Not Routinely Evaluate Its Program Effectiveness

Collecting feedback on the program from both the participant and host agency supervisor perspectives can help to build on lessons learned and improve the program. As of 2010, the POLAD program began to collect feedback on its orientation sessions. The program also solicits feedback annually from incumbent POLAD participants in order to improve the position descriptions. More recently, POLAD program management developed informal written guidance to improve the performance appraisal process for POLAD participants while on rotation at DOD commands, using input from internal experts. Program management maintains frequent communication with both participants and their host agencies, which according to a State official, helps them to make changes to POLAD positions as the need arises. However, program officials acknowledged that an overall evaluation of program effectiveness, taking into account both the participant and host supervisor perspectives, has not been conducted. The majority of POLAD participants and host supervisors that responded to our survey indicated that they had not been asked to complete an evaluation of the program (see figure 7).

Figure 7: Responses of POLAD Participants and Host Supervisors to the Question "Did you have an opportunity to complete an evaluation or provide feedback on the interagency rotational assignment program in some formal way?"

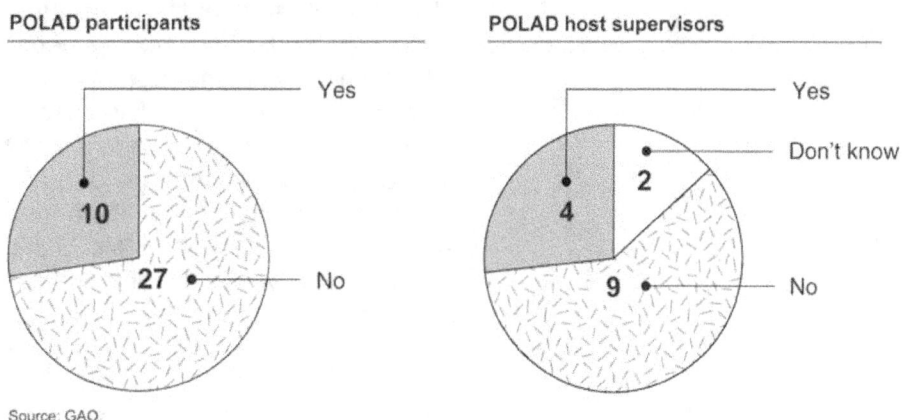

Source: GAO.

A POLAD program official said that the increasing demand for the program—significantly more applicants as well as a greater number of DOD requests to host POLADs—provide key indicators of the program's success. However, routine program evaluation information that takes into account various aspects of the program may help POLAD program management to build on specific strengths and to identify areas for improvement.

State's Other Interagency Rotations Were Not Specifically Designed to Achieve Interagency or Department-Level Strategic Goals

Similar to the POLAD program discussed above, State officials said that the QDDR, a high-level foreign policy document, provides the rationale for these assignments, with its emphasis on the importance of interagency experience and rotations in improving engagement and coordination with other agencies. In addition, the QDDR signals State's intent to expand its use of interagency rotations as a means of achieving specific national security goals as well as building its human capital. However, whereas the POLAD program is linked to specific Political-Military Bureau goals, State human resources officials acknowledge that there are currently no agency-level plans that indicate how these assignments are used to further the Department's strategic goals.

State human resources officials explained that these other interagency assignments have evolved individually over time to meet agency needs and are therefore not managed together as a program of rotations. One official noted that the National Security Professional Development (NSPD) initiative, which involved multiple agencies, could have served as a framework for these rotations.[22] This official acknowledged that since NSPD is currently focused on emergency management, which is outside of State's central mission, State is seeking another approach to managing these interagency assignments to achieve strategic goals.

State officials said that they view these interagency rotation assignments as an important means for the Department to build and sustain relationships with other agencies in the national security arena. They also noted that the number of such assignments is likely to increase in response to the growing recognition that interagency collaboration is needed to accomplish many of State's missions. However, by not explicitly planning for how these assignments could be used to achieve shared national security goals, State may be missing opportunities to fully leverage positive results of these assignments, for both the participating individuals and agencies.

---

[22]Executive Order 13434, May 17, 2007, entitled National Security Professional Development, required the heads of all agencies with national security responsibilities to identify or enhance current professional development activities for their national security personnel. 72 Fed. Reg. 28,583 (May 17, 2007). Several agencies, including State, developed implementation plans for training and other developmental activities. More recently, in 2011, the Obama administration has shifted NSPD to specific mission areas, with emergency management as the initial focus.

State Provided Few Incentives for Civil Service Personnel to Participate In Other Interagency Rotations

Unlike the POLAD program discussed above, which seeks to recruit participants exclusively from the Foreign Service, participants of State's other interagency rotations include civil service personnel as well as Foreign Service Officers. According to a State human resources official, while historically, most of these assignments have been filled by Foreign Service Officers, civil service participation in these assignments can be valuable to both the individual and the Department. However, civil service personnel are not provided with incentives to participate in these types of assignments and may even face challenges to participation, as noted in the QDDR. According to this document, "talented Civil Servants have also been victims of their own success: opportunities for mobility at State…[have] been limited by the indispensable role they often play in their existing positions, making supervisors reluctant to release them for extended training or rotational assignments."

While revisions to the Foreign Service competencies may provide incentives for Foreign Service Officers to participate in these assignments, there have been no similar revisions to the civil service competencies. With the exception of a "partnering" competency for the senior executive service, there are no competencies related directly to collaboration or interagency experience although one official said that State is considering revising these in the future.

In addition, State does not publicly recognize participants of these rotations as a means of encouraging others to participate. Although State has an extensive award system in place, officials acknowledged that it does not address how excellent performance in an interagency rotation should be taken into account when considering employees for awards. Further, because these interagency rotations are managed individually, these officials said that there are no practices in place to recognize participants through presentations or briefings, or similar opportunities. Accordingly, only 3 of the 24 participants responding to our survey agreed that "Participants are publicly recognized and rewarded (for example, through announcements, awards, etc.) at my home agency."

Without adequate participation incentives—or with the perception of inadequate incentives—State's civil service personnel may be discouraged from applying to interagency rotations. For example, if potential participants are concerned that an interagency rotation could slow their career progression, State may only attract candidates nearing retirement, which would make it difficult for State to capture the benefits of the participants' gains in interagency knowledge, skills, or networks.

State Has Not Provided Incentives for Its Supervisors to Support Civil Service Rotations but Has Provided Some Incentives for Host Agencies

As noted in the section on POLADs above, some of the common disincentives for home-agency supervisors to support their staff in going on an interagency rotation are not relevant for Foreign Service Officers. However, these incentives are relevant for State supervisors of civil service personnel, who may be left with difficult-to-cover gaps while staff are on rotation at another agency. We found that State does not provide incentives, or take other steps to mitigate disincentives for supervisors of civil service personnel to let staff go on rotations. According to a State human resources official, supervisors are responsible for ensuring that their subordinates have appropriate developmental opportunities. However, State doesn't use its performance management system to set expectations that supervisors are to share their human resources through interagency rotations, which, according to our analysis, is one way to provide incentives. A State official indicated that the department is considering an assessment of its civil service competencies, which could allow them to incorporate interagency experience and collaboration skills. They may also begin to use individual training and development plans for more of their civil service personnel. These changes could provide incentives for supervisors to send staff on rotations, if their individual development plans indicated the need for interagency experience. This official acknowledged, however, that moving forward with the new competency assessment is dependent upon availability of resources. In the absence of such performance management policies and practices, supervisors may not support their staff going on interagency rotations, even when they could benefit participants and agencies. As a result, State could miss opportunities to achieve collaboration-related results at both the individual and organizational level.

We also found that State provides other agencies with incentives to host its rotational staff by taking steps to ensure high-performing candidates are provided. Host agencies play a role in the selection of participants for interagency rotations ranging from requesting specific candidates to choosing candidates that applied for the rotation and were selected by a panel of Foreign Service Officers.

State Accounted for Host Agency Needs and Participant Development Goals in Making Interagency Rotation Assignments

For interagency rotations that fall outside of the POLAD program, State has policies and practices in place to ensure that host agencies' needs are met in matching applicants to assignments. According to State human resources officials, participant recruitment and selection procedures vary depending on the host agency and type of assignment. For example, for senior-level rotations to National Defense University, the military services' war colleges, and other federal agencies, interested personnel bid on the positions and are preliminarily selected by the leadership of State's Bureau of Human Resources. Candidates are then referred to the host agencies for their concurrence. For mid-level rotations to federal agencies and other organizations, review panels are convened to consider applications and develop a rank-order list. Finalists are then referred for host-agency concurrence. In some cases, such as rotations to the National Security Staff, the host agency requests specific candidates.

To ensure that the rotation will address a participant's developmental needs, applications for these interagency rotations include a statement of their qualifications, how the developmental experience fits their career objectives, and how it would benefit the department.

State Has Not Established Practices to Prepare Participants or Host-Agency Supervisors of Other Interagency Rotations

Unlike the POLAD program, with its formal orientation training and materials, State human resources officials said there is no such preparation for participants of its other interagency rotations, which are managed individually. Accordingly, most participants responding to our survey (21 of 24) indicated that they did not take part in an orientation or training. Further, in responding to a survey question on what information might have been useful in preparation for the rotation, 11 participants did have suggestions, with most of these asking for more advance information on the host-agency or responsibilities.

Selected Survey Responses from Other State Interagency Rotation Participants on Information That Would Have Been Useful to Prepare Them

"anything that would have prepared me not to fly by the seat of my proverbial pants."

"I would strongly recommend an in-house seminar of a week or two's duration for personnel embarking on a rotational assignment to ensure that personnel have a consistent, accurate understanding of their agency's roles and missions."

"Orientation to how [the host] is organized prior to arrival would have been very beneficial."

"More information about the responsibilities of the assignment...."

Source: GAO survey responses.

In addition, State human resources officials said that they do not provide formal guidance or preparatory materials to the host agency. These officials explained that many of these interagency rotations are long-established and that it is common for host-agency supervisors to have significant prior experience in managing the rotations and therefore do not need to be prepared. This may be why none of the 14 host-agency supervisors responding to our survey commented that there was a need for preparatory information.

We reviewed examples of MOUs that govern these rotations but none of them provided instruction for discussing developmental goals or setting performance expectations for the participants, which is an important part of preparing both participants and their supervisors. However, our survey results indicated that this may be taking place in many cases without guidance or instruction: most participants (16 of 24) and host-agency supervisors (13 of 14) reported communications on expectations or goals. Nevertheless, pre-rotation preparation could help participants learn to navigate in the new organization more efficiently and enable participants and supervisors to establish a common understanding of what each hopes to gain from the rotation earlier in the process.

State Relied on Civil Service Participants to Plan for Effective Use of Knowledge, Skills, and Networks Gained on Interagency Rotations

According to State human resources officials, for the small number of civil service personnel that currently participate in interagency rotations, the Department does not have a process to ensure that the knowledge, skills, and networks that they gained on interagency rotations are used upon their return.[23] Civil service participants are responsible for discussing with their supervisors how their post-rotation responsibilities will build on their rotation experience. However, these officials said that they do ensure that there are open lines of communication between State and the participants while they are away, to help participants to keep abreast of new

---

[23]These interagency rotations are open to both Foreign Service and civil service personnel, although at present, there are relatively few civil service participants. As noted earlier, because State's Foreign Service career development and staffing model is beyond the scope of this report, we did not evaluate the effectiveness of how State planned for its Foreign Service participants' next assignments.

developments and career opportunities. While on rotation, participants receive Department notices via email on a daily basis, as well as access to State's internal personnel and other information systems. This continued access is important, officials explained, because State personnel rely on their professional networks within the Department as a way of advancing their careers in the direction that benefits them.

State human resources officials said that because in the past, the number of civil service personnel participating in these interagency rotations had been small, it did not make sense to establish post-rotation planning practices for so few participants. However, the QDDR specifically describes goals to increase civil service participation in interagency rotations and other key assignments. If the small number of civil service participants grows, the lack of post-rotation planning practices could cause State to miss opportunities to leverage participants' developmental gains.

State Did Not Routinely Collect Feedback to Evaluate the Effectiveness of Other Interagency Rotations

State human resources officials indicated that they collect informal feedback on its other interagency rotations for the purpose of determining whether to maintain or cut future positions. These officials acknowledged that they do not routinely collect or evaluate information from participants or host-agency supervisors on rotation outcomes or other elements that could be used to improve how future rotations are managed. Survey responses are consistent with this, with the majority of participants (21 of 24) and half of host supervisors (7 of 14) responding to our survey reporting that they had not been asked to complete an evaluation of the rotation. Officials said that, historically, they have not managed these rotations as they would manage a program and therefore had not considered evaluating it as such. However, without regular feedback on the rotations from participants and their host agency supervisors, the agency may be missing opportunities to identify and address potential challenges to the effectiveness of these rotations.

CGSC Interagency Fellowship Program Was Designed to Achieve Army's Collaboration-Related Leadership Development Goals

Our review of the CGSC Interagency Fellowship program design and relevant planning documents indicated that the program was developed as part of the Army's larger goals for developing its leadership. According to a CGSC program official, the idea for the Interagency Fellowship program was originated as part of the Leader Development and Education program within the Army Training and Doctrine Command, who approved and enabled CGSC to execute it.[24] Specifically, the program was designed to provide an experience to "broaden the understanding of the complex Joint, Interagency, Intergovernmental, and Multinational environment in which the Army operates with its national security partners," which aligns with the Army's leadership development goals as described in its strategic plan. In addition, samples of the memorandums of agreement (MOA) between the Army and other agencies participating in the program indicate that the program has been positioned to achieve results for all those involved. For example, the MOA with the U.S. Marshals Service (USMS) acknowledges that participants' experiences "will benefit the Army by enhancing understanding and familiarity with the interagency process and USMS practices and policies" and outlines the structure of the program in the context of meeting this goal.

CGSC Provided Prospective Interagency Fellows with Incentives to Participate

We found that the CGSC Interagency Fellowship program employed a number of performance management and other practices that provided incentives to participate during the 2009 program year we reviewed, and has continued to strengthen incentives since then. Moreover, we found that the number of applicants to the program has increased.

- Participants' performance while on rotation was included in their formal performance appraisals. In 2009, according to CGSC officials, host agency supervisors were encouraged to complete an Officer Evaluation Report for their Fellows. According to our survey results, 100 percent (16 of 16) of the 2009 Fellows who responded to our survey question on this topic indicated that their performance while on rotation was included in their formal appraisal. Most of these respondents (14 of 16) reported that their performance while on rotation was given sufficient merit in their formal performance appraisal. More recently, in 2011, to ensure participant performance

---

[24]The U.S. Army Training and Doctrine Command, known as TRADOC, is responsible for developing, educating, and training Army soldiers, civilians, and leaders, among other responsibilities.

during the rotation is appraised and documented, program officials have made completion of an Officer Evaluation Report mandatory for the host agency supervisors.

- Early on in the program, officials acknowledged the Fellows by publishing their names on program marketing materials. In 2010, program officials introduced a requirement for Fellows to write a paper on their interagency experience and said that they would seek to publish some of these. While the purpose of the papers was to ensure that education and development takes place in conjunction with the completion of the mission at the host agency, publishing these will also serve as a means of publicly recognizing the Fellows for their work while on interagency assignment.

- In 2011, the Fellowship was approved as a means for participants to earn certain Joint Professional Military Education credits toward joint officer qualification and competitive status for promotion.[25]

CGSC Sought to Encourage Host Agencies to Participate by Providing High-Performing Participants and Clarifying Agencies' Roles and Responsibilities

CGSC program officials seek to work through any potential governance issues that could be cumbersome for host agencies or that could discourage their participation using MOAs to detail roles and responsibilities.[26] For example, the MOAs address which agency will be responsible for salaries and any additional costs; how participants will be selected; performance accountability provisions; security clearance requirements; among other considerations. In addition, program officials sought to attract and retain host-agency participation by adopting several practices to ensure the highest-performing applicants were selected. The Fellowship positions are posted through a standard military personnel message. Applicants are selected through a review board, which is instructed to identify the highest performers. According to documentation Army Human Resources Command (HRC) provided to us, in fiscal year 2011, 140 officers applied to the program to compete for 28 available

---

[25]CGSC Fellowship meets joint officer Joint Professional Military Education Phase 1 credit, which supports fulfillment of the educational requirements for joint officer management. Successful completion of the course also provides participants Military Education Level 4 credit, which offers officers a competitive status for promotion.

[26]Because most participants of the CGSC Interagency Fellowship program go on rotations after attending military academic education, rather than directly from a performing unit, we did not assess whether incentives are provided to Army supervisors to support their staff going on a rotation.

positions, which, according to program officials, allowed them to select "the best and the brightest." Moreover, 11 of 12 of the CGSC host supervisors responding to our survey were either very satisfied or somewhat satisfied with the quality of the participants.

CGSC Program Employed Mechanisms to Help Match Needs of Participants and Host Agencies

The CGSC Interagency Fellowship program has mechanisms in place to help create a good match between the participant and assignment by using information about both individual developmental needs and the host-agencies' organizational needs. The CGSC application process encourages participants to describe their individual development goals and professional interests. In addition, according to the MOA, the host agency is to detail the specific skills and capabilities it requires from participants. Of the participants and supervisors who responded to our survey, the majority were either very or somewhat satisfied with the match. Specifically, 13 of 16 participants and 11 of 12 supervisors were either very or somewhat satisfied with the match between the participant's abilities and the assignment.

Selected Survey Responses From CGSC Fellowship Host Supervisors

"[The Army Command and General Staff College's Interagency Fellowship is] a truly inspired idea that addresses a fundamental deficiency in our government's approach to problems requiring inter-agency solutions. Needs to be furthered and developed in the selection and matching process and the evaluation process."

"The success of the program depends on the quality of the person doing the rotation. We were very fortunate with MAJ [redacted]. There is a significant amount of training time necessary for the individual before they can be a productive member of this office. If they are highly qualified and motivated, this training is worth the effort. The program was an excellent opportunity for both sides to gain an understanding of how the other organization in the USG operates."

Source: GAO survey responses.

The Army CGSC Interagency Fellowship Program Prepared Participants for Some Aspects of the Program but Did Not Prepare Host Supervisors

The CGSC Interagency Fellowship program began to provide orientation training for participants at the beginning of the 2011 program year. Topics included information on the program's background and objectives, how the rotation fits in with CGSC's academic requirements, CGSC's expectations of each participant, the selection process, among others. However, the orientation materials did not include information intended to prepare the participants to work at a specific host agency, such as information on host-agency authorities and capabilities. Program officials said that they had designed the program to require the host-agency to provide their own orientation training to familiarize participants with their organizational environment. For example, the MOA with the USMS requires them to provide "initial orientation to USMS operational processes and procedures." These officials explained that they did not want to supplant the host-agency's expertise in providing relevant information on their own organization. Further, these officials noted that because program participants may be selected before the details of the assignments are finalized, they do not always know which units will be hosting the participants or who their supervisors will be at the time that they are providing their orientation session.

Because our survey was administered to 2009 participants and host-agency supervisors, the responses do not reflect the most current program practices. Nonetheless, we include them since they may be useful in guiding the topics and the breadth of information covered in current orientation or other training materials. Of the responding fiscal year 2009 participants that did receive training (2 of 16) or written materials (5 of 16)—which may have come from the host agency—several indicated they did not receive sufficient information that would have been useful to them on the following topics: the process for selecting participants for a rotation (3 of 6); the process for appraising their performance during the rotation (3 of 6); the process for transitioning to their next assignment (4 of 6); and how to optimize their experience during the assignment (5 of 6). In addition, open-ended responses indicated that participants responding to our survey would have liked information on (1) what the Interagency Fellowship program expected the participants to accomplish and (2) information on the host agency unit's mission and goals. The Interagency Fellowship program's recently-established orientation seems intended to address the former information. However, the MOA requirement that host-agencies provide orientation may not be enough to ensure that participants on rotations at various agencies are consistently receiving the host-agency-specific preparation they need. In responding to open-ended survey questions, three participants indicated they would have liked more information on the host agency's mission and goals, while four indicated that their host agency offered such information. Without such preparation, participants may not be able to contribute to the host agency—or to their own professional development—as effectively as possible.

According to CGSC Interagency Fellowship program officials, they use the MOAs governing these rotations to communicate information that the host-agency supervisors need to manage the rotation. Our review of examples of MOAs indicated that these include information on the overall purpose of the rotations, performance appraisal mechanisms, and other information that is useful in preparing host-agency supervisors. In addition, program officials said that they instruct participants to meet with their supervisors at the start of the rotation to explain the program requirements. However, we reviewed examples of MOAs and the content was focused primarily on agency-level roles and responsibilities and did not discuss how the Interagency Fellowship was to serve as a developmental experience for the participant, which may have been helpful in preparing host-agency supervisors. According to our survey results, only 4 of 12 host-agency supervisors responding to our survey indicated that they received written materials intended to help prepare them to host a participant. One host supervisor suggested in an open-ended response that additional information on the goals and expectations of the program would have been useful. In addition, according to written participant feedback that program officials obtained in 2010, 9 of 19 participants recommended that the program should provide clearer guidance to the host agencies concerning the program's objectives and expectations for what the participants should gain from the program. Without comprehensive guidance—to clarify the host-agency supervisor's role in managing the rotation to help the participant to achieve developmental goals as well as mission goals—supervisors may not be prepared to manage rotations to achieve the greatest possible benefits.

The CGSC Interagency Fellowship Program Plans for Participant's Next Assignment

Army Regulations which govern numerous Army fellowship and scholarship programs, include policies and procedures for participants' follow-on assignments to ensure that the Army obtains maximum benefit from its investment.[27] While some Army programs require specific follow-on assignments in which the benefits of the education will be used immediately upon completion, CGSC officials said that the Interagency Fellowship program is seen as a long-term investment in officer careers. If the immediate post-rotation assignment does not fully leverage participants' interagency experience, future assignments are likely to include joint interagency positions, which would allow the Army to benefit from the knowledge, skills, and networks acquired. Furthermore, they explained that they do not require specific follow-on assignments because these could interfere with officers completing "Key Developmental" assignments needed for promotion, which could discourage participation in the program.[28]

Another way the CGSC Fellowship seeks to leverage the knowledge that participants gain during their interagency rotation is through a newly established writing requirement. The program has added a learning component in which participants are required to write a paper suitable for publication on their experience during the fellowship. The purpose of the papers is to ensure that education and development takes place in conjunction with the completion of the mission at the host agency. If published, participants can share their experience and knowledge of the interagency environment.

While participants meet with program managers regularly, the program managers are not responsible for coordinating post-program assignments. Rather, they are coordinated by career managers in HRC. Participants are provided contact information for HRC and post-program assignments are discussed during the participant's orientation. Most CGSC participants responding to our survey (15 of 16) reported having

---

[27] Army Regulation 621-7, *Army Fellowships and Scholarships* (Aug. 8, 1997). The CGSC Interagency Fellowship was established in 2010, after the most recent version of Army Regulations 621-7, so it is not currently incorporated in the regulations. Army officials stated that they have submitted draft guidance on the program for inclusion in a revised regulation and are currently operating under the draft guidance provided to GAO.

[28] A Key Developmental assignment is considered fundamental to the development of an officer and in providing experience across the Army's strategic mission.

discussed their transition to a new assignment or their return to their home agency while they were still on rotation.

The CGSC Interagency Fellowship Program Did Not Routinely Collect Feedback to Evaluate Program Effectiveness

As noted above, collecting feedback on the program from both the participant and host agency supervisor perspectives helps to build on lessons learned and improves the program. CGSC program officials seek mid-year program feedback from participants each year. Although the request for feedback is informal and collected along with other information not directly related to evaluating the program, program officials reported that they used the information to modify program processes and educational certifications. Specifically, program officials seek feedback from participants on what areas could be improved in the program. A program official said that 20 of 22 participants told him they would repeat the Fellowship if offered the opportunity again. As reported earlier, our survey corroborated the participants' largely positive perspectives on the program.

As shown in figure 8, half of the participants responding to our survey indicated that they did not have the opportunity to complete an evaluation or provide formal feedback on the interagency rotation program. However, in 2010 the program began to assess participant learning outcomes by requiring participants to write a paper. This new requirement may offer some insight into the participants' perspectives of their developmental outcomes. This is a first step in understanding the programs' impact on participant learning outcomes. However, officials do not evaluate the outcomes either for host agencies or for the Army. Program officials acknowledged that they do not routinely collect feedback from host agency supervisors, although they do make an effort to meet with as many as they can throughout the program year. Half of the CGSC supervisors responding to our survey (6 of 12) reported having an opportunity to complete an evaluation or provide feedback on the interagency rotation program in some formal way.

Figure 8: Responses of CGSC Participants and Host Supervisors to the Question "Did you have an opportunity to complete an evaluation or provide feedback on the interagency rotational assignment program in some formal way?"

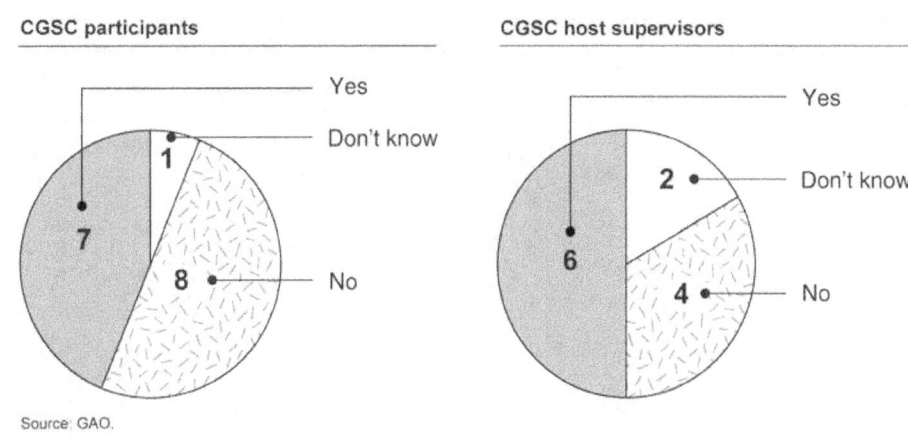

Source: GAO.

Conclusions

Interagency rotation programs can build individual and institutional capacity to collaborate, which has become increasingly important in the complex national security arena of the 21st century. Both State and DOD have signaled they intend to increase their use of interagency rotations as a tool to achieve common national security goals. State's POLAD program and other interagency rotations as well as the Army CGSC Interagency Fellowship demonstrate how rotations benefit everyone involved—participants and supervisors we surveyed mostly agreed that collaboration-related results were achieved. Our analysis suggests that addressing various program design and management challenges—such as inadequate preparation or failure to obtain feedback from all parties involved—can further strengthen the effectiveness of such programs. While the programs we looked at have incorporated many of the policies and practices that contribute to effective rotations, each could improve collaboration-related results by adopting additional policies and practices. For example, each of the programs could benefit from a more formal approach to evaluating program effectiveness. State's other interagency rotations, which have not been managed as a single program, could also benefit from improved preparation as well as post-rotation planning and stronger incentives for civil servants to participate, if State moves forward with plans to increase its use of civil service personnel in these areas. Building on good policies and practices that have been established, as State and Army CGSC seek to expand these programs and assignments, it will become more important to ensure that effective policies and

GAO-12-386 Interagency Collaboration

practices are in place to help achieve these programs' wide-reaching mission, developmental, and collaboration-related goals.

Recommendations for Executive Action

To improve the effectiveness of the POLAD program as a tool to facilitate interagency collaboration on national security, we recommend that the Secretary of State direct the Bureau of Human Resources and the Office of the Coordinator of the Foreign Policy Advisor (POLAD) Program to take the following action:

- Expand the scope of current efforts by routinely evaluating the effectiveness of the program to determine if desired results are being achieved for participating individuals and agencies, to identify and build on areas of strength, and to identify areas for improvement.

To improve the effectiveness of State's interagency rotations to other government agencies and federal learning institutes as tools to facilitate interagency collaboration on national security, we recommend that the Secretary of State direct the Bureau of Human Resources to take the following three actions:

- Clarify agency plans for how these assignments will contribute to achieving shared national security goals. For example, State could use strategic workforce planning to determine the current and future positions needed to accomplish its collaboration-dependent goals and that would benefit from interagency rotations. Such plans should also address the extent to which civil service personnel will participate in interagency rotations.

- Work with host agency counterparts to develop orientation materials that would help both participants and host agency supervisors to maximize the benefits from the rotation. Such materials could include, for example, information on the goals of the interagency rotation, the roles and responsibilities of the host agency and the participant, administrative details, and tips and best practices for a successful rotation.

- Routinely evaluate the effectiveness of the program to determine if desired results are being achieved for participating individuals and agencies, to identify and build on areas of strength, and to identify areas for improvement.

Further, depending on whether State determines that it will increase civil service participation in other interagency rotations as a means to achieve goals set forth in the QDDR, we recommend that the Secretary of State direct the Bureau of Human Resources to take the following three actions:

- Improve incentives for civil service personnel to participate in interagency rotations by providing guidance to supervisors on how to consider interagency experience and collaboration abilities when assessing civil service personnel with national security responsibilities for performance ratings and awards. Guidance could also include suggestions for how to publicly recognize returning participants' interagency experience through presentations, briefings, or other high-profile opportunities.

- Improve incentives for supervisors to support civil service personnel's participation in interagency rotations, if such participation would help State meet national security and workforce development goals, by establishing performance expectations that supervisors share human resources, as appropriate.

- Develop guidance for State supervisors of civil servants who are assigned to an interagency rotation on how to ensure that the knowledge, skills, and networks gained during the rotation are used to the extent possible upon their return.

To improve the effectiveness of the Army's CGSC Interagency Fellowship Program as a tool to facilitate interagency collaboration on national security, the Secretary of Defense should direct Fellowship program officials to take the following two actions:

- Building on existing MOA requirements, work with host agency counterparts to develop orientation materials that would help host supervisors to maximize the benefits from the rotation for both the participant and the host agency. Such materials could include, for example, information on the goals of the interagency rotation, the roles and responsibilities of the host agency and the participant, administrative details, and tips and best practices for a successful rotation.

- Routinely evaluate the effectiveness of the program to determine if desired results are being achieved for participating individuals and agencies, to identify and build on areas of strength, and to identify areas for improvement.

Agency Comments and Our Evaluation

We provided a draft of this report to the Secretaries of State and Defense for their review and comment. Both State and DOD provided written comments which are reproduced in appendixes III and IV. They also provided technical comments that were incorporated throughout the report, as appropriate.

State generally agreed with our recommendations. In our draft report, we recommended that the Secretary of State direct the Bureau of Human Resources and the Office of the Coordinator of the POLAD program to work with DOD counterparts to develop orientation materials that would help POLAD host supervisors to maximize the benefits from the rotation for both the participant and the host agency. After we provided the draft report to State, the department provided us with a PowerPoint briefing for host agency supervisors at the DOD commands that POLAD program management had recently developed. The department also provided evidence that POLAD program management is seeking to identify and contact new host agency supervisors with background information about the POLAD program and offering additional information or materials. As a result of these actions, we revised our finding and removed the relevant recommendation from the final report.

In response to our recommendation that it work with host agencies to develop additional orientation materials, State noted that in many cases there is one employee going to each host agency and said that it would have to weigh the costs and effort of producing and maintaining orientation materials for many such small-scale rotations. However, there are some simple and cost-effective steps that State can take to develop orientation materials, such as creating PowerPoint briefing slides like those it created for POLAD program supervisors as described above.

DOD concurred with our recommendations and described several steps that it will take to implement the recommendations. These steps include working with partner agencies to build additional orientation materials, requiring participants in the Interagency Fellowship Program to send a synopsis of lessons learned and best practices in quarterly updates, and conducting follow-up surveys to capture longer-term results of program participation.

We are sending copies of this report to the Departments of State and Defense, and other interested parties. In addition, the report is available at no charge on the GAO website at http://www.gao.gov.

If you or your staff have any questions about this report, please contact me at (202) 512-6806 or mihmj@gao.gov. Contact points for our Offices of Congressional Relations and Public Affairs may be found on the last page of this report. GAO staff who made key contributions to this report are listed in appendix V.

J. Christopher Mihm
Managing Director, Strategic Issues

List of Requesters

The Honorable Susan M. Collins
Ranking Member
Committee on Homeland Security and Governmental Affairs
United States Senate

The Honorable Daniel K. Akaka
Chairman
Subcommittee on Oversight of Government Management, the Federal
Workforce, and the
District of Columbia
Committee on Homeland Security and Governmental Affairs
United States Senate

The Honorable Jason Chaffetz
Chairman
The Honorable John F. Tierney
Ranking Member
Subcommittee on National Security, Homeland Defense and Foreign
Operations
Committee on Oversight and Government Reform
House of Representatives

The Honorable Jeff Flake
House of Representatives

Appendix I: Objectives, Scope, and Methodology

To better understand how to effectively design and implement interagency rotation programs, this report addresses the following research objectives: (1) identify desirable collaboration-related results of interagency rotation programs in terms of individual competencies and organizational results; (2) identify policies and practices that help interagency rotation programs achieve collaboration-related results; and (3) determine the extent to which interagency rotation programs we identified in our previous report,[1] were viewed as effective and incorporated those policies and practices.

To address objectives 1 and 2, we developed criteria for desirable outcomes and effective policies and practices by drawing on three sets of sources as described below.

- **Literature:** A range of published books, articles, and working type papers from U.S. and international business and other academic journals and public policy research institutes.

- **External experts:** Human capital and training and development professionals from outside of the agencies we reviewed, with expertise on rotations or similar professional development programs.[2]

- **Agency practitioners:** Federal human capital and training and development professionals at 9 agencies with national security responsibilities that were selected based upon our previous report.

We collected this information through a series of interviews, a questionnaire, and a literature review. We analyzed the results of each of these three methods and developed the criteria as described below.

Literature review

We conducted an extensive literature review to identify collaboration-related outcomes that can be achieved through effective rotation programs, as well as policies and practices that can facilitate or challenge the effectiveness of such programs in achieving key collaboration-related

---

[1]GAO, *National Security: An Overview of Professional Development Activities Intended to Improve Interagency Collaboration*, GAO-11-108 (Washington, D.C.: Nov. 15, 2010).

[2]In selecting external experts, we reviewed their biographical information to determine whether they were likely to have personal or financial impairments that could potentially impair their opinions.

outcomes. We employed several approaches to identify relevant literature, including (1) a formal search conducted by a GAO research librarian; (2) literature recommendations from external experts and agency practitioners we interviewed; and (3) materials collected during the team's background research from internal stakeholders and elsewhere. Our formal search included several databases and limited results to articles, trade publications, dissertations, books and other working type papers published in the last 15 to 20 years. In addition to the database searches, we reviewed publications recommended by experts we interviewed as well as those we identified conducting our own background research. This search yielded hundreds of documents, which were further narrowed using professional judgment to include only those that focused on discussions of criteria for successful programs and described lessons learned or best practices. As part of our search criteria, we also sought publications that examined outcomes or practices associated with joint duty assignments following the implementation of the Goldwater-Nichols Act[3] because their findings may be relevant to interagency rotations. In general, however, we did not use the type of organizations or policy arena as an exclusionary criterion. If it was clear how the policies, practices, or possible outcomes could be applied to job rotation programs in the federal national security arena, we included them in our selection for in-depth analysis. For example, we did not exclude publications that focused on the human services policy arena or the manufacturing sector simply because their context was not identical to that of the federal national security arena. With these criteria, we reviewed the abstracts of 189 publications and selected 56 publications to review in depth. For each article, we identified any positive or negative collaboration-related outcomes of rotations as well as policies and practices that facilitate or challenge effective job rotations.

---

[3]The Goldwater-Nichols Department of Defense Reorganization Act of 1986 was enacted, in part, to improve officers' professional development through education in joint matters and assignment to joint organizations. The act further requires DOD to factor this joint education and experience into its officer promotion decisions. Pub. L. No. 99-433 (Oct. 1, 1986).

External Experts: Content Analysis of Interview Summaries

To help ensure that the policies, practices, outcomes, and challenges for effective job rotation programs that we identified were objective and reflected a range of perspectives, we sought referrals from human capital and professional development practitioners at GAO and from professional associations, such as the National Academy of Human Resources and the National Academy for Public Administration, and other experts to identify external experts and interviewed 13 that represented a range of corporate, academic, and public sector perspectives. Two analysts independently reviewed the content of the interview summaries to categorize each comment as a type of positive or negative rotation outcome, or associated policy, practice, or challenge. Where the two analysts' judgment differed, a third analyst reviewed the category assignment to render a decision. In some cases, differences in judgments were resolved through discussion among the three analysts.

Agency Practitioners: Interviews and Follow-Up Questionnaire

To ensure that we obtained the perspectives of agency practitioners, we built on our recent work on a related topic, which included interviews with human capital or professional development practitioners at 9 federal agencies with national security responsibilities, including: the Departments of Commerce, Homeland Security, Defense (including the National Defense University), Justice (including the Federal Bureau of Investigation and the Bureau of Alcohol, Tobacco, Firearms, and Explosives), State, Treasury, Agriculture, Energy; and the U.S. Agency for International Development.[4] We conducted a content analysis of these interviews to preliminarily identify desirable outcomes, policies, practices, and challenges associated with interagency rotations. We used this information to develop a questionnaire to obtain agency practitioners' perspectives on each item and to elicit any additional information that we had not already identified during past interviews. We refined the questionnaire by pretesting it via email with experts from the study population. On April 18, 2011, we emailed the questionnaire to 49 agency practitioners that we had previously interviewed[5], in the form of a Microsoft Word document that respondents could return electronically

---

[4]See GAO-11-108, appendix I, which describes our methodology for selecting the agencies and the agency officials we interviewed.

[5]If the previously interviewed practitioner was no longer available (i.e., had left the agency), we asked the agency to designate another practitioner with the same or similar responsibilities, and sent the questionnaire to the new designate instead.

after entering responses into open answer boxes. Ten days later, we sent a reminder letter to everyone who had not responded, and another reminder after 3 weeks. We received 34 questionnaires by May 17, 2011, for a final response rate of 69 percent. The questionnaire results are provided in appendix II.

Criteria Development

From the results of the three analyses above, we identified (1) collaboration-related outcomes that can be achieved by rotation programs; (2) policies and practices that contribute to or challenge the achievement of collaboration-related outcomes; and (3) potential questions or topics to include in our participant and supervisor survey. We reviewed the results of the three analyses for consistency across all sources, and for both unique and contradictory information. In determining whether each outcome, policy or practice is appropriate for use as a criterion, we considered how frequently it was cited, its prevalence across the different sources, and whether the policy or practice is actionable in the federal government sector. We included a cited outcome, policy or practice as a criterion if it met the following conditions: (1) it was represented in at least two of the three sets of sources, or if cited in a single source type it was represented by at least 80 percent of agency practitioners, two external experts, or three sources of literature; and (2) it was feasible to adopt the practice in the federal government sector (e.g., we excluded granting stock options for performance rewards). Finally, in order to identify criteria that are broadly applicable, we took steps to aggregate similar themes. We categorized each item into both large groups and subgroups, and then discussed these groupings as a team until we arrived at a consensus that each item had been categorized and aggregated appropriately.

To address objective 3, we began a preliminary review of the seven interagency rotation programs we identified in our prior report.[6] We excluded four of these programs that were newly established and/or those that targeted participants without prior professional experience, such as military school cadets, since it would be difficult to gauge whether these programs had contributed to organizational results or to participants' professional development.

---

[6]In GAO-11-108, we identified interagency rotational assignment programs that were intended to improve national security collaboration while providing professional development opportunities for its participants.

After selecting the Department of State's (State) Foreign Policy Advisor
(POLAD) Program, State's other interagency rotations, and the
Department of the Army's Command and General Staff College's (CGSC)
Intermediate Level Education Interagency Fellowship Program for our
review, we looked at relevant agency-level and program-level
documentation. These included:

- High-level policy and planning documents, such as the Quadrennial
  Diplomacy and Development Review and the U.S. Army Strategic
  Planning Guidance.

- Program documentation such as the POLAD handbook and the
  directives establishing the CGSC Interagency Fellowship and its
  program requirements.

- Documentation specific to the interagency rotation, such as vacancy
  announcements and interagency agreements that governed the
  assignments.

We conducted interviews with the program managers and human capital
officials for each of the three programs; and administered surveys to all
fiscal year 2009 program participants, their host agency supervisors, and,
if appropriate, their supervisors prior to the interagency rotation.[7] We
selected the survey participants from a single fiscal year to provide a
snapshot of the outcomes the programs have achieved and the policies
and practices in place. To best capture the most recent information from
participants and supervisors that had completed the programs, we
selected fiscal year 2009 participants and supervisors because these
rotations were more likely to have been completed at the time of the
surveys than those of fiscal year 2010. Program officials provided contact
information for all fiscal year 2009 participants and both their pre-rotation
supervisors and host supervisors. We reviewed the information for
completeness and duplicates and followed up as necessary to obtain the
most complete and accurate information. Some participants and
supervisors had retired since the rotation or their information was not
available, so we excluded them from the population. Some supervisors

---

[7]CGSC program officials confirmed that program participants do not typically have a pre-
rotation supervisor, but rather an academic advisor because they are taking courses prior
to their rotation. Therefore, we did not include these supervisors in our population for the
pre-rotation supervisor survey.

GAO-12-386 Interagency Collaboration

managed more than one participant, so rather than sending multiple surveys to those supervisors, we selected one of the participants for them to consider as they responded to the survey. Likewise, some participants had more than one rotation during the study period, so where possible, we chose the most recent rotation.

We obtained sufficient contact information for 55 of 72 participants from State's POLAD program, for 49 of 59 participants from State's other interagency rotations, and for 20 of 23 participants from CGSC's Interagency Fellowship program. For these 124 participants, we received sufficient information for 58 of 105 pre-rotation supervisors and 85 of 124 host supervisors.

Table 1 shows the response rate for each survey and the total survey population. Responses to the pre-rotation supervisor survey were not sufficient (21 of 58) to include in the report. Participants responding to the survey were assigned to various host agencies, including the Departments of Defense, State; and the U.S. Agency for International Development, among others. Host supervisors responding to our survey were from several agencies, including the Departments of Defense, State, the Executive Office of the President, and the U.S. Agency for International Development, among others. We conducted a non-response bias analysis based on home agency and program and found that there was some bias. Therefore, the results may only reflect the views of the survey respondents and not all participants or host supervisors.

Table 1: Response Rates to Surveys by Program

	Program			Total Responses	Initial Survey Sample[a]
	CGSC Interagency Fellowship	State POLAD	Other State Rotations		
Participants	16 of 20 (80%)	37 of 55 (67%)	24 of 49 (49%)	77 (62%)	124
Host Supervisors	12 of 17 (71%)	15 of 42 (36%)	14 of 26 (54%)	41 (48%)	85
Pre-rotation Supervisors	N/A	11 of 35 (31%)	10 of 23 (43%)	21 (36%)	58

Source: GAO.

[a]Does not include participants or supervisors for which we did not have contact information, were retired, or otherwise inelig ble for inclusion.

The questions for each survey were developed based on the criteria developed as described above to determine respondents' perspectives on the extent to which each program achieves the desirable outcomes and has adopted effective policies and practices. Before distributing the

surveys online, we revised them to reflect comments from an independent
reviewer within GAO. We revised the surveys again after we further
pretested the surveys via phone and online with three participants, two
host supervisors, and two prior supervisors from the study population. We
conducted pretests to make sure that the questions were clear and
unbiased and that the questionnaire did not place an undue burden on
respondents. The web-based surveys were administered from mid-
September 2011 to mid-October 2011. Respondents were sent an e-mail
invitation to complete the survey on a secure GAO web server using a
unique username and password. Throughout the data collection period,
nonrespondents received reminder e-mails and phone calls.

We followed-up with some respondents to clarify their responses
regarding the program they participated in during fiscal year 2009. We
had reason to believe that not all respondents understood the strict
definition of the programs, so in some cases , we reassigned these
participants to the appropriate program based on follow-up conversations,
their responses to open-ended questions, and information from program
officials defining the programs. In addition, we omitted responses to some
questions where respondents answered questions they should have
skipped based on previous responses. All data analysis programs were
independently verified for accuracy. The surveys and their data used for
this study are available at http://www.gao.gov/products/GAO-12-387SP.[8]

To evaluate the extent to which each program had the above-mentioned
desirable policies and practices in place, we reviewed all three sources of
information (documents, interviews, and survey results). As described in
our report, these policies and practices can be implemented using a
number of methods we identified. An analyst looked for evidence that the
programs had each of the policies and practices in place, using some or
all of the methods, as applicable, and assigned a rating as follows:

- Policies and practices mostly or fully in place, represented by a full
  circle: we found most or all methods of implementing the policy and
  practice were fully in place;
- Policies and practices partially in place, represented by a half circle:
  We did not find that most or all methods of implementing the policy

---

[8]GAO, *Interagency Collaboration: National Security Rotation Programs Need Incentives,
Preparation, and Feedback, an E-supplement to GAO-12-386*, GAO-12-387SP
(Washington, D.C.: Mar. 9, 2012).

and practice were fully in place, but did find that at least some methods were partially in place; or

- Policies or practices not in place, represented by an empty circle: we found no methods of implementing the policy and practice in place.

A team of analysts then reviewed the evidence used to make the initial ratings and discussed them to arrive at a consensus.

We conducted this performance audit from February 2011 to March 2012 in accordance with generally accepted government auditing standards. Those standards require that we plan and perform the audit to obtain sufficient, appropriate evidence to provide a reasonable basis for our findings and conclusions based on our audit objectives. We believe that the evidence obtained provides a reasonable basis for our findings and conclusions based on our audit objectives.

Appendix II: Results from GAO's Questionnaire on Desirable Outcomes and Effective Policies and Practices Associated with Interagency Rotation Programs

The following questionnaire was administered to human capital or professional development practitioners at nine federal agencies with national security responsibilities, including: the Departments of Commerce, Homeland Security, Defense (including the National Defense University), Justice (including the Federal Bureau of Investigation and the Bureau of Alcohol, Tobacco, Firearms, and Explosives), State, Treasury, Agriculture, and Energy; and the U.S. Agency for International Development.[1] The questionnaire we administered is reproduced below with the results for each question.

Background: Last year, as part of a review of national security-related professional development activities, GAO interviewed human capital, training, education, and other officials at numerous federal agencies and federal learning institutes. Agency officials provided, among other things, their perspectives on policies and practices that can either promote or challenge the effectiveness of interagency rotation programs in improving interagency collaboration. You are receiving this questionnaire because you or your agency participated in these interviews.

Purpose of this questionnaire: As part of this ongoing body of work, GAO is refining its understanding of the policies and practices that are related to effective interagency rotation programs. GAO is asking you to review a list of policies and practices that were identified in the original interviews and rate their importance in promoting or challenging program effectiveness.

Instructions: Please review the following list of policies and practices. Part 1 contains policies and practices that were mentioned as promoting the effectiveness of rotation programs in facilitating interagency collaboration, while Part 2 contains policies and practices that were mentioned as challenging the effectiveness of such programs. Please indicate your opinion of each policy or practice by placing an "X" or other mark in one of the boxes on each row.

One of our goals is to compile a list of policies and practices that is **as comprehensive as possible**. For this reason, we are including an open-ended question at the end of each part of the questionnaire. Please use

---

[1]See GAO-11-108, appendix I, which describes our methodology for selecting the agencies and the agency officials we interviewed.

Appendix II: Results from GAO's
Questionnaire on Desirable Outcomes and
Effective Policies and Practices Associated
with Interagency Rotation Programs

these questions to describe any additional policies or practices that might promote or challenge the effectiveness of interagency rotation programs in facilitating interagency collaboration.

Contact information: GAO staff contact information appeared here.

Definitions/Key:

FS: Foreign Service

G/FO: General/Flag Officer

Home agency: the agency at which the participant is normally employed, sometimes referred to as the sending agency.

Host agency: the agency at which the participant is temporarily assigned, sometimes referred to as the gaining agency.

O: officer level

Rotational assignments: for the purposes of this document, these refer to interagency assignments across departmental or independent agency lines, rather than assignments from one component agency to another component agency.

SES: Senior Executive Service

SFS: Senior Foreign Service

Part I: Policies and Practices Identified by Agency Officials as Promoting the Effectiveness of Interagency Rotation Programs in Facilitating Interagency Collaboration

For each statement below, please select the option that best describes your views. Select "very" important to indicate that the item is critical to a program's effectiveness in facilitating interagency collaboration or "somewhat" important if the item is desirable but not critical. Select "not" important if the item is irrelevant to a program's success.

Appendix II: Results from GAO's
Questionnaire on Desirable Outcomes and
Effective Policies and Practices Associated
with Interagency Rotation Programs

Table 2: Percentage Responses to Part I of Questionnaire

Question	Not important	Somewhat important	Very important	Don't know / no opinion
Desired Program Outcomes				
1. Rotational assignments should have clearly defined outcomes.	0%	24%	76%	0%
2. The host agency should benefit (e.g. be able to achieve mission objectives more effectively) from the knowledge, skills, etc. participants bring to the assignment.	3%	38%	59%	0%
3. By the end of the rotation, participants should have improved their skills and knowledge.	3%	3%	94%	0%
4. By the end of the rotation, participants should have developed a network of contacts, professional relationships at other agencies.	3%	24%	74%	0%
5. By the end of the rotation, participants should have gained in-depth knowledge of the host agency.	3%	32%	65%	0%
6. The home agency should benefit (e.g. be able to achieve mission objectives more effectively) from the knowledge, skills, networks, etc. that participants have acquired during rotational assignments.	3%	15%	82%	0%
Program Design				
7. All relevant stakeholders (e.g. home and host agencies) should be involved in designing rotational assignment programs.[a]	0%	12%	88%	0%
8. Rotational assignments should provide developmental opportunities for individual participants AND help the host agency meet its mission responsibilities.	3%	26%	71%	0%
9. A rotational assignment program should be part of a larger talent management or workforce development plan.	6%	38%	56%	0%
10. A rotational assignment program should include an upfront agreement for what participants' responsibilities will be during the assignment.	3%	24%	71%	3%
11. The home agency should have a plan in place for how to use participants' newly acquired skills, knowledge, or networks upon their return.	9%	24%	68%	0%
Pre-Rotation Preparation				
12. Training or guidance on how to represent the home agency, expectations, logistics, etc., should be provided to participants before the assignment begins.	3%	38%	59%	0%
13. Orientation training on the host agency's organizational structure, mission, and responsibilities, etc. should be provided to participants.	6%	21%	74%	0%
14. Training or guidance should be provided for host agency supervisors on expectations, logistics, etc.	0%	32%	68%	0%

Appendix II: Results from GAO's
Questionnaire on Desirable Outcomes and
Effective Policies and Practices Associated
with Interagency Rotation Programs

Question	Not important	Somewhat important	Very important	Don't know / no opinion
15. Guidelines and/or mechanisms for periodic communication between participants and their home agencies should be provided.	0%	38%	62%	0%
16. A cohort or community of practice for rotating personnel and a means for them to communicate with one another should be established.	15%	50%	35%	0%
Participant Selection/Assignment Selection				
17. Information on rotational assignment opportunities should be widely publicized to prospective participants.	6%	9%	82%	3%
18. Participants should be selected competitively.	18%	29%	44%	9%
19. Participants should be selected on the basis of excellence in past job performance.	18%	29%	50%	3%
20. Participants should be selected based on their potential as future leaders in the national security community.	12%	29%	56%	3%
21. Participants should be selected because their individual development plans (or similar information) indicate that a rotational assignment would develop needed skills.	12%	56%	29%	3%
22. Participants should be selected based on their ability to contribute to the host agency.	3%	71%	24%	3%
23. Rotational assignment programs should target participants at the executive level (i.e. SES, SFS, G/FO, or equivalents.)	32%	44%	24%	0%
24. Rotational assignment programs should target participants at the mid- to senior level (i.e. GS-12-15, FS 4 – 1, O4 – O6, or equivalent)	9%	35%	53%	3%
25. The rotational assignment should make use of participants' knowledge or skills.	6%	41%	53%	0%
26. Participants should be placed in assignments that are relevant for future interagency collaborative efforts.	0%	21%	79%	0%
27. The rotational assignment should provide participants with a "stretch" opportunity to improve knowledge or skills.	6%	26%	68%	0%
Individual and Organizational Participation Incentives				
28. To encourage agencies to participate, top administration leadership should demonstrate its commitment to the rotational assignment program.	6%	9%	85%	0%
29. To encourage its personnel to participate, top agency leadership should demonstrate its commitment to the rotational assignment program.	3%	0%	97%	0%
30. Upon successful completion of the assignment, participants that have performed well should be assigned to positions that are desirable and/or career-enhancing.	6%	38%	56%	0%

**Appendix II: Results from GAO's
Questionnaire on Desirable Outcomes and
Effective Policies and Practices Associated
with Interagency Rotation Programs**

Question	Not important	Somewhat important	Very important	Don't know / no opinion
31. Participants' newly-acquired experience, knowledge, etc. should be publicly recognized by agency/organization leadership (e.g. through brief-back opportunities at leadership meetings, newsletter articles, awards, etc.).	15%	38%	47%	0%
32. Rotational assignments should be required for promotion to senior level positions.	9%	47%	35%	9%
33. The home agency should have a strategy for covering participants' home-agency responsibilities during the assignment.	0%	21%	76%	3%
34. The home agency should have mechanisms for retaining participants after they return from assignment (e.g. continuing service agreements, etc.).	0%	29%	68%	3%
Performance Management				
35. Performance appraisal systems should have a mechanism for capturing host-agency supervisor performance feedback.	3%	12%	85%	0%
36. Performance appraisal systems should have a mechanism for rewarding successful performance at other agencies.	6%	29%	65%	0%
37. Participants' should be held accountable for improving their performance in competency areas related to their rotational assignment.	6%	41%	53%	0%
Program evaluation				
38. Agencies should have mechanisms for evaluating the success of rotational assignment programs in achieving desired outcomes.	3%	9%	88%	0%
39. Agencies should obtain feedback on rotational assignment programs from various stakeholders, such as host agency supervisors, home agency line managers, participants, etc.	3%	6%	91%	0%
40. Please use the space below to describe any additional policies and practices that you consider important to the effectiveness of interagency rotational programs in facilitating interagency collaboration	Responses intentionally not reported			

Source: GAO.

Note: Unless otherwise indicated, the number of responses to each question is 34.

[a]There were 33 responses to this question.

Appendix II: Results from GAO's
Questionnaire on Desirable Outcomes and
Effective Policies and Practices Associated
with Interagency Rotation Programs

Part II: Policies and Practices Identified by Agency Officials as Challenging the Effectiveness of Interagency Rotation Programs in Facilitating Interagency Collaboration

For each statement below, please select the option that best describes your views. Select "very" challenging to indicate that the item could cause a program to fail or "moderately" challenging if the item could limit a program's effectiveness in facilitating interagency collaboration. Select "not" challenging if the item is irrelevant to a program's success.

Table 3: Percentage Responses to Part II of Questionnaire

Question	Not challenging	Moderately challenging	Very challenging	Don't know / no opinion
Program Development Process				
1. Participating agencies lack resources to take part in designing or implementing a rotational assignment program.	6%	26%	59%	9%
2. Inability to share funds can discourage human capital leadership from collaborating with other agencies on the design and implementation of rotational assignment programs.	9%	26%	41%	24%
Program Design/Assignment Duration				
3. It is difficult for participants to make a meaningful contribution to a host agency during a short-term (less than six months) rotational assignment.	38%	41%	21%	0%
4. Home agencies view long-term rotations, which require their personnel to be away for more than six months, as a significant resource burden.	3%	26%	71%	0%
Individual and Organizational Disincentives for Participation				
5. Lack of centralized information on rotational assignment opportunities in the national security arena is a barrier to participation.	15%	26%	47%	12%
6. Prospective participants are concerned that home agency managers will discount their performance and developmental experiences at the host agency.	9%	35%	44%	12%

**Appendix II: Results from GAO's
Questionnaire on Desirable Outcomes and
Effective Policies and Practices Associated
with Interagency Rotation Programs**

Question	Not challenging	Moderately challenging	Very challenging	Don't know / no opinion
7. Prospective participants are concerned that their promotion prospects will be diminished as a result from being away from the home agency.	9%	29%	47%	15%
8. In the case of a rotation exchange, agencies or supervisors are concerned about lack of equity (i.e. one agency sends a high performer and another agency sends a low performer).	15%	56%	12%	18%
9. Home agencies or supervisors are concerned that host agencies will "poach" high-performing rotational assignment participants.	9%	65%	12%	15%
10. The home agency has no means of covering participants' responsibilities during rotational assignments.	6%	26%	62%	6%
Funding and staffing allocation rules				
11. Incremental TDY costs result from assigning personnel from a geographically inexpensive area to a higher-expense area (e.g. from a field office location at one agency to a D.C. headquarters location at another agency).	15%	41%	29%	15%
12. There are no established interagency policies on funding for rotational assignments (e.g. rules for TDY reimbursements or other agreements).	18%	38%	29%	15%
13. Funding rules make interagency personnel exchanges and other reimbursement or cost-sharing mechanisms difficult.	15%	38%	38%	9%
14. Limits to FTE levels make it difficult for the home agency to back-fill positions while personnel are on rotational assignment. 1	6%	24%	58%	12%
15. Please use the space below to describe any additional policies and practices that you consider a challenge to the effectiveness of interagency rotational programs in facilitating interagency collaboration	Responses intentionally not reported			

Source: GAO.

Note: Unless otherwise indicated, the number of responses to each question is 34.

[a]There were 33 responses to this question.

Appendix III: Comments from the Department of State

United States Department of State

Chief Financial Officer

Washington, D.C. 20520

Mr. Loren Yager
Managing Director
International Affairs and Trade
Government Accountability Office
441 G Street, N.W.
Washington, D.C. 20548-0001

MAR - 2 2012

Dear Mr. Yager:

We appreciate the opportunity to review your draft report, "INTERAGENCY COLLABORATION: State and Army Rotation Programs Can Build on Positive Results with Additional Preparation and Evaluation," GAO Job Code 450883.

The enclosed Department of State comments are provided for incorporation with this letter as an appendix to the final report.

If you have any questions concerning this response, please contact Bert Curtis, HR Policy Specialist, Office of the Director General, Bureau of Human Resources at (202) 647-2655.

Sincerely,

James L. Millette

cc: GAO – Bernice Steinhardt
     DGHR– Steven A. Browning
     State/OIG – Evelyn Klemstine

Department of State Comments on GAO Draft Report

<u>**INTERAGENCY COLLABORATION:** State and Army Rotation Programs
Can Build on Positive Results with Additional Preparation and Evaluation</u>
(GAO-12-386, GAO Code 450883)

The Department thanks GAO for its evaluation of the interagency rotations cited in
this report. We were pleased to note that of the job rotation programs cited for
"improving interagency national security collaboration" studied in 2009 - 2010 and
published in "National Security: An Overview of Professional Development
Activities Intended to Improve Interagency Collaboration," GAO chose to closely
examine the Department of State offerings (POLAD and other agency job
rotations) in this follow-on review. We note that GAO found that these rotations
exhibited most of the best practices they determined to be useful in their earlier
work.

Just as it is a key part of the culture of the Foreign Service that officers and
specialists move from diplomatic post to diplomatic post, our employees embrace
the challenge and the privilege of being immersed in and contributing to another
organization's operations and culture. We agree with GAO that such experiences
are invaluable for the Department, for the host organization and for the individuals
involved. The Department welcomes the opportunity to sustain and improve the
quality of interagency rotations, which date back to the first POLAD on record,
who served with General Eisenhower during World War II. We take seriously
GAO's interest in further strengthening these programs and will consider their
recommendations, with which we agree in principal, very carefully.

**<u>Recommendation Regarding Orientation Materials for Other Agency
Rotations</u>**
GAO suggests that the Department might further strengthen the other agency
rotations by developing additional orientation materials for participants and host
supervisors. While we agree that such material might contribute to the success of
the rotation, we note that rotations to other agencies pose practical challenges,
since, in many cases, there is one employee going to each host agency. The
Department would have to weigh the costs and effort of producing and maintaining
orientation material for many such small-scale rotations. As part of an over-all
analysis of the Department's rotations (see below), we will consider the question of
what types of orientation materials might be necessary, appropriate and cost-
effective and design them accordingly.

2

Recommendations Regarding Evaluation of POLAD and Other Agency Rotations

The Department agrees that it is important to take stock of and evaluate our existing inter-agency rotations. We are fortunate to have a robust menu of inter-agency rotational opportunities and a workforce that is eager to accept the challenges posed by the myriad assignment possibilities. Furthermore, when such rotations are part of an exchange relationship, (i.e., employees also rotate from other agencies into the State Department) the "winnings" are amplified.

As part of the first phase of the Quadrennial Development and Diplomatic Review, (QDDR) implementation, a working group in the Bureau of Human Resources has developed a consolidated listing of our incoming and outgoing details and will create a data base and tools to track assignments and evaluate the effectiveness and overall benefits of details to the Department, the participating employees and the host agencies. At that time we expect to be able to regularly evaluate details both individually and collectively in line with our strategic objectives.

Recommendation Regarding Clarification of How Other Interagency Rotations Contribute To Achieving Shared National Security Goals

We agree with GAO that each of the reviewed rotations can and should contribute to achieving shared national security goals. The clear mission of the Department of State, writ large, is the promotion of national security. As described in the report, the National Security Professional Development (NSPD) Initiative could have served as a framework for these rotations. By definition, every Foreign Service Officer *is* a national security professional and every U.S. foreign mission is an inter-agency environment. The inclusion of interagency experience in the Foreign Service precepts is evidence of the fact that, ideally, every Foreign Service Officer would have the experience described in this GAO report in order to be better prepared for the challenges of working with interagency colleagues, though we realize that this is impractical. Regarding the Civil Service, we explain below the nature of our current expansion of Civil Service opportunities.

Recommendations Regarding Civil Service Participation in Job Rotations

In the event that the Department determines that we are ready and resourced to increase Civil Service participation in inter-agency rotations, we will utilize GAO's recommendations regarding incentives and guidance for employees and their supervisors. GAO notes that the QDDR calls for increased developmental opportunities for our Civil Service workforce. To help fill staffing gaps while providing Civil Service employees a broader perspective of our foreign policy

3

mission when they return to domestic positions, we are placing emphasis at this time on overseas developmental opportunities within the Department.

The Department recently established the Office of Overseas Civil Service Assignments (OCSA). This office has initiated a pilot project utilizing USAJOBS and merit promotion regulations to allow Civil Service employees to compete for overseas positions and possible promotion. These assignments will normally have two-year duration. Early response to the overseas excursion pilot has been favorable, with numerous Civil Service applicants for the initial round of overseas positions. While the rules of the Civil Service do not offer the flexibilities afforded by the rules of the Foreign Service, we are committed to exploring ways to allow and encourage our Civil Service employees to contribute their skills and knowledge in new environments. If we do expand inter-agency rotations, we will be able to utilize the lessons learned from this initiative.

Response Summary

In 2010, CENTCOM's General David Petraeus gave a presentation to the Department which was broadcast to our employees worldwide. He stated that rotation programs are, "…essential in carrying out whole-of-government endeavors…throughout the world." Again, the Department appreciates GAO's interest in this area, which we believe is vital as we continue to seek to put the right people in the right place at the right time with the right skills.

Appendix IV: Comments from the Department of Defense

OFFICE OF THE UNDER SECRETARY OF DEFENSE
4000 DEFENSE PENTAGON
WASHINGTON, D.C. 20301-4000

FEB 2 8 2012

PERSONNEL AND
READINESS

Mr. J. Christopher Mihm
Managing Director, Strategic Issues
U.S. Government Accountability Office
441 G Street, NW
Washington, DC 20548

Dear Mr. Mihm:

This is the Department of Defense's response to the Government Accountability Office (GAO) Draft Report, GAO-12-386, "INTERAGENCY COLLABORATION: National Security Rotation Programs Need Incentives, Preparation, and Feedback," dated February 3, 2012 (GAO Code 450883).

The Department concurs with the enclosed recommendations as stated in the GAO Report. We reviewed the comments from the collateral action offices and have summarized the suggestions coupled with the agreed-to actions that the Department believes will remedy the short falls identified in the Report.

The Directorate of Officer and Enlisted Personnel Management will be the primary action office for this action. Thank you for your review of this program and assistance in making it a more productive and effective learning environment for the Department.

Sincerely,

Virginia S. Penrod
Deputy Assistant Secretary
(Military Personnel Policy)

Enclosure:
As stated

GAO DRAFT REPORT DATED FEBRUARY 3, 2012
GAO-12-386 (GAO CODE 450883)

"INTERAGENCY COLLABORATION: NATIONAL SECURITY ROTATION
PROGRAMS NEED INCENTIVES, PREPARATION, AND FEEDBACK"

DEPARTMENT OF DEFENSE COMMENTS
TO THE GAO RECOMMENDATIONS

To improve the effectiveness of the Army's CGSC Interagency Fellowship Program as a tool to facilitate interagency collaboration on national security, the GAO recommends that the Secretary of Defense should direct Fellowship program officials:

RECOMMENDATION 1: Building on existing MOA requirement, to work with host agency counterparts to develop orientation materials that would help host supervisors to maximize the benefits from the rotation for both the participant and the host agency. Such materials could include, for example, information on the goals of the interagency rotation, the roles and responsibilities of the host agency and the participant, administrative details, and tips and best practices for a successful rotation.

DoD RESPONSE: Concur.

DoD Action Plan: The Command and General Staff College (CGSC) will continue to work with partner agencies to refine existing orientations materials to better prepare agency supervisors and Interagency Fellows for the program. These materials will expand on existing guidance in the MOA's and will provide more detail information on desired outcomes for both the agencies and the Fellows. For the Fellows, CGSC will expand the briefing on the goals and their responsibilities for the Fellowship program at the beginning of the Intermediate Level Education (ILE) Core course which they attend prior to their Fellowships. CGSC will continue to maintain regular contact with them for periodic updates on their status throughout their Fellowship assignment. CGSC will work with agency partners to expand upon their existing orientation seminars and classes to better target the fellows needs. CGSC will also continue to solicit feedback from the Fellows at the middle and at the end of their Fellowship assignment.

For the agency supervisors, CGSC will provide additional information and descriptions on the purpose, goals, and support requirements for the Fellowship Program. This will include, but will not be limited to, additional guidance on the Officer Evaluation System, periodic direct contact with Fellowship Program management, and request for end-of-tour Lessons Learned submissions. This will be accomplished via e-mail, teleconferences, and face-to-face meetings.

CGSC will work to build the additional materials starting with one major partner, the Department of State, with the Fall of 2012 as a target date for completion. CGSC will expand that to include as many of our partner agencies as possible by the Fall of 2013.

MOAs represent a successful foundation for rotational assignments implemented in accordance with the IC Civilian Joint Duty Program. Delineating roles and

responsibilities and administrative details are effective for the employee and those
managing and/or overseeing the employee's assignment. Information regarding the
successful implementation of the assignment may be conveyed during an overarching
orientation in preparation of the individual's assignment.

Building on existing MOA requirement, to work with host agency counterparts to
develop orientation materials that would help host supervisors to maximize the benefits
from the rotation for both the participant and the host agency. Such materials could
include, for example, information on the goals of the interagency rotation, the roles, and
responsibilities of the host agency and the participant, administrative details, and tips and
best practices for a successful rotation.

RECOMMENDATION 2: Routinely evaluate the effectiveness of the program to
determine if desired results are being achieved for participating individuals and agencies,
to identify and build on areas of strength, and to identify areas for improvement.

DoD RESPONSE: Concur.

DoD Action Plan: The Command and General Staff College (CGSC) Intermediate
Level Education (ILE) Interagency Fellowship Program managers will expand on the
requirement for all Fellows to write a paper on three program learning outcomes by
implementing a quarterly Lessons Learned program. Each Fellow will send a synopsis of
lessons learned and best practices as quarterly updates for program management to
consolidate, vet and redistribute to all Fellows. These quarterly updates will enable better
evaluation of the effectiveness of the program and will form the basis for a history of
lessons learned to be made available for future Fellows.

In addition and working with officials at the U.S. Army Human Resource Command,
Interagency Fellowship Program managers will work to create a personnel tracking
identifier, either a Special Skill Identifier or an additional Skill Identifier, to track all
officers who have served as ILE Interagency Fellows under the program. This will be
done retroactively as well for all current and future Fellows. The intent of this identifier
is to allow program management to track follow-on assignments and for allowing surveys
at the 1 year and 5 year points following the Fellowship assignment. Surveys, designed
to capture longer-term results of program participation for both the Fellows and the
Army, will be sent to former Fellows and current supervisors at the 1 and 5 year points.
The secondary benefit of this identifier will be to allow Army leadership to quickly tap
into the special experience and knowledge the Fellows gain about the agencies they
served in for future whole-of-government operations. The timeline for these
improvements will be to complete all of the above during the next Fellowship year
starting in FY12.

2

Appendix V: GAO Contact and Staff Acknowledgments

GAO Contact	J. Christopher Mihm at (202) 512-6806 or mihmj@gao.gov
Staff Acknowledgments	Elizabeth Curda and Laura Miller Craig managed this assignment. Russ Burnett, Jessica Nierenberg, Melanie Papasian, Erin Saunders Rath, Albert Sim, and Kate Hudson Walker made key contributions to all aspects of the report. Judith Kordahl, Jill Lacey, Marie Mak, John Pendleton, Sonya Phillips, Lindsay Read, and Megan M. Taylor also provided assistance. In addition, Karin Fangman and Lois Hanshaw provided legal support and Donna Miller developed the report's graphics.

Related GAO Products

Humanitarian and Development Assistance: Project Evaluations and Better Information Sharing Needed to Manage the Military's Efforts. GAO-12-359. Washington, D.C.: February 8, 2012.

Department of State: Additional Steps Are Needed to Improve Strategic Planning and Evaluation of Training for State Personnel. GAO-11-241. Washington, D.C.: March 8, 2011.

National Security: An Overview of Professional Development Activities Intended to Improve Interagency Collaboration. GAO-11-108. Washington, D.C.: December 15, 2010.

Defense Management: Improved Planning, Training, and Interagency Collaboration Could Strengthen DOD's Efforts in Africa. GAO-10-794 Washington, D.C.: July 28, 2010.

National Security: Interagency Collaboration Practices and Challenges at DOD's Southern and Africa Commands. GAO-10-962T. Washington, D.C.: July 28, 2010.

Defense Management: U.S. Southern Command Demonstrates Interagency Collaboration, but Its Haiti Disaster Response Revealed Challenges Conducting a Large Military Operation. GAO-10-801. Washington, D.C.: July 28, 2010.

National Security: Key Challenges and Solutions to Strengthen Interagency Collaboration. GAO-10-822T. Washington, D.C.: June 9, 2010.

Defense Management: DOD Needs to Determine the Future of Its Horn of Africa Task Force. GAO-10-504. Washington, D.C.: April 15, 2010.

Homeland Defense: DOD Needs to Take Actions to Enhance Interagency Coordination for Its Homeland Defense and Civil Support Missions. GAO-10-364. Washington, D.C.: March 30, 2010.

Interagency Collaboration: Key Issues for Congressional Oversight of National Security Strategies, Organizations, Workforce, and Information Sharing. GAO-09-904SP. Washington, D.C.: September 25, 2009.

Military Training: DOD Needs a Strategic Plan and Better Inventory and Requirements Data to Guide Development of Language Skills and Regional Proficiency. GAO-09-568. Washington, D.C.: June 19, 2009.

Influenza Pandemic: Continued Focus on the Nation's Planning and Preparedness Efforts Remains Essential. GAO-09-760T. Washington, D.C.: June 3, 2009.

U.S. Public Diplomacy: Key Issues for Congressional Oversight. GAO-09-679SP. Washington, D.C.: May 27, 2009.

Military Operations: Actions Needed to Improve Oversight and Interagency Coordination for the Commander's Emergency Response Program in Afghanistan. GAO-09-61. Washington, D.C.: May 18, 2009.

Foreign Aid Reform: Comprehensive Strategy, Interagency Coordination, and Operational Improvements Would Bolster Current Efforts. GAO-09-192. Washington, D.C.: April 17, 2009.

Iraq and Afghanistan: Security, Economic, and Governance Challenges to Rebuilding Efforts Should Be Addressed in U.S. Strategies. GAO-09-476T. Washington, D.C.: March 25, 2009.

Drug Control: Better Coordination with the Department of Homeland Security and an Updated Accountability Framework Can Further Enhance DEA's Efforts to Meet Post-9/11 Responsibilities. GAO-09-63. Washington, D.C.: March 20, 2009.

Defense Management: Actions Needed to Address Stakeholder Concerns, Improve Interagency Collaboration, and Determine Full Costs Associated with the U.S. Africa Command. GAO-09-181. Washington, D.C.: February 20, 2009.

Results-Oriented Government: Practices That Can Help Enhance and Sustain Collaboration among Federal Agencies. GAO-06-15. Washington, D.C.: October 21, 2005.

Human Capital: A Guide for Training and Development Efforts in the Federal Government. GAO-04-546G. Washington, D.C.: March 2004.

Human Capital: Key Principles for Effective Strategic Workforce Planning. GAO-04-39. Washington, D.C.: December 11, 2003.

Please Print on Recycled Paper.